# APPALACHIAN CONJURING

100 Spells, Conjurings, Healings and

Folk Practices from Modern Day

Appalachian Witches And

Granny Women Magick Decedents

Ashley Conner

Misty Conner

Ronda Caudill

Copyright © 2023

## Conner, Conner & Caudill

All rights reserved. No part of this book may be reproduced in any manner whatsoever without written consent from the author. This book is a work of fiction and should not be construed as real. The names, characters, places, and incidents are products of the author's imagination. Any similarities to a person's (living or dead), actual events, locations and organizations are entirely coincidental.

ISBN: **9798390524299**

# DEDICATION

Ashley, Misty, and Ronda would like to dedicate this book to all of those who have come before them on this path of enlightenment, who have called themselves healers, heathens, witches, and everything in between.

These beautiful Appalachian Mountains they call home have given birth to many beautiful creatures but those with the gift of magick is the most beautiful of all.

They hope that all who read this collection of their stories, spells and conjurings that they have shared enjoy the magick that has been handed down through their families and they have cultivated in their own practices.

*The mountains were calling, stoic and grand and holding within them mysteries of eons spun into a thriving tapestry, landscapes as much emotional as biological or cultural. I could see all the layers breathing in unison, and I knew I had returned home.*

*-Adam Daniel*

# CONTENTS

| | | |
|---|---|---|
| | Acknowledgments | i |
| 1 | Our home, the Appalachian Mountains | 1 |
| 2 | What is a Granny Woman? | 15 |
| 3 | Word to the Wise ~Caution~ | 27 |
| 4 | Ashley Conner's Magick | 29 |
| 5 | Ashley's Workings | 37 |
| 6 | Misty Conner's Magick | 105 |
| 7 | Misty's Conjurings | 111 |
| 8 | Ronda Caudill's Magick | 206 |
| 9 | Ronda's Spells | 211 |
| 10 | 100th Spell | 248 |
| 11 | Appalachian Superstition | 249 |
| 12 | Ronda's Superstitions | 249 |
| 13 | Misty's Superstitions | 256 |
| 14 | Appalachian Lore (Ashley) | 261 |

# ACKNOWLEDGMENTS

We would like to thank our families because without them we would not be here today with this strong lineage and moxie for life.

~Merry Meet~

# OUR HOME, THE APPALACHIAN MOUNTAINS

As we describe the place we call home, I believe no words could justify its beauty, dangers and enchantment all wrapped up into one unless you experience it yourself. The next best thing that could be done to give you the full experience we encounter every day would be to let you see it from our eyes. These words will never live up to what you feel in the Appalachian because it isn't just about looks and touch, it is about the energy that is captured in what seems to be a time capsule in these mountains which is isolated from the hustle and bustle of everyday normal life of our current society.

These Mountains have stood tall and towering over many a creature that have graced this little planet we inhabit. The mountains themselves were created roughly 480 million years ago, being among some of the oldest, with heights that were taller than the Alps and Rocky Mountains. When we think of this time span, to really understand and grasp the meaning, this was long

Appalachian Farm in the moonlight

before any human stood in the Appalachian shadows of today because it was under water. Fossils can be found of sea creatures of long ago before man was even a glimpse on the horizon. As they emerged and became land, these mountains held the secrets of time within them. With these towering shadows that are casted, it is hard to believe the Appalachians

Photo courtesy of Ecoclimax

have shrunk with erosion, at one time it is thought they were much taller, so tall as to even rival Mt. Everest in heights.

What calls people to these historic structures is also a feeling of home, even if you have never stepped foot in this region. This is a very understandable feeling because before our world was formed as it is now, it was one large land mass, Pangea. The Appalachians at that time were apart of Africa, and Europe. As the continents divided, the roots of those long-separated lands still have an energy here. It also made it an understanding home to future generations for immigrants that would flow into these hillside and mountain tops.

As the world was growing and being founded, Spanish explorers found a village of Native Americans in upper Florida, who's name they believed to be Apalchen or Apalachen with the Spanish and Native American influences not only was the name given to the tribe but also the region. Later, it would be adapted to the current spelling, Appalachian and current location. Along with all of the other remarkable things held in these lands that you will hear briefly about; the name is the fourth oldest European named location in the US.

Detail of Gutierrez' 1562 map showing the first known cartographic appearance of a variant of the name "Appalachia."

Some of the locations on these hillsides and mountain tops are still uninhabited today, but back when immigrants began to move into this country, it was an unforgiving terrain for some. The complexity was night and day in comparison. You had the harsh terrain, unbearable weather and an uncivilized society, but on the other hand, remarkable beauty, natural environmental resources, and freedom. The first to embrace this land was Native Americans, numerous tribes were blended into the fabric of these mountains. As time came for new settlers, some of the first was the Scotch-Irish, German and the most overlooked is those of African lineage. The one thing that set the Southern Appalachian apart from the regular thought of the South that people overlooked was the landscape. Plantations with vast lands were more towards the flat lands, which meant the mountains were freedom and safety for numerous groups. The rich fertile soil of the south was not lost to the mountains, but a different mindset was needed to make it grow and bloom. A different mindset was indeed what was needed and what most had because, being of numerous minority groups that came to this country seeking refuge, they felt at home because the mountains had a similar terrain that they came from. The one thing society and mainstream are good at is pushing those they deem unworthy or lower class away, they put them somewhere out of sight, in this case it was the mountains.

People often can hear a person from the Appalachian before they even see them because of their pronunciations and dialect. Just as we have mentioned, this time capsule is determined to keep the old traditions alive, and our communication skills is among the most unique. People often think when they hear a southern Appalachian talk that they are ill-educated or "backwoods," so much so that numerous famous people coming from this region have chosen to adapt their speech to more conventional ways. When we deep dive into our speech we understand it is actually quite different than what people expected, it is more authentic to our native tongues of our homelands. You will find many of us, and definitely our elders, will put "a" in front of their verbs such as "a-going" that is a direct line to their lineage. The twang and the usage of certain dialects can be traced to the proper way of speech for many immigrants. So, what people see as a weakness to a social standing is actually a lineage that still honors the old traditions of a time long ago.

The blending of these lineages happened very quickly because survival was needed, not by just one group but by all. Each ethnic group brought something unique, such as the Scotch-Irish had the clan mentality and their pride. They kept their loved ones close, such as in the hollers you may find generations after generation living in close proximity to each other. As you travel these hillsides, it was common for the families to stick together even on issues that may affect only one family member, this being the epitome of clan mentality. Two incredibly famous families that represent this are the Hatfields and McCoys.

Photo courtesy Visit Pikeville

As the melting pot of minorities grew, so did their abilities to adapt,

A TYPICAL MALUNGEON.

not to mention the Native American influences in the form of most of the lineages eventually have a trace of Indigenous bloodlines or the knowledge of them passed down through families by word of mouth. This unique blending gave birth to something most unusual, an Indigenous tribe all of our own, the Melungeons. This bloodline has always thought to be of Indigenous origin because of the skin color which is normally more of an olive complexion and sometimes lighter eyes. As more information has come out overtime, the tribe has strong African and European roots. As the times were changing, many tried to pass as European in nature but also of Portugal descent. Now the pride of this lineage is protected and documented by the Melungeon Heritage Association.

As time marched on, the mountain people kept to themselves until things became known that could benefit society outside of the confinements of these towering mountains, our natural resources, and the most notable was coal. Most of the families residing in the Appalachian region had a history of not trusting the government or society because of having to flee from persecution in some form which lead them to what they called home now, only to be taken advantage of again by large corporations that came in with what sounded like a new way of life for the average man. The coal industry left the towns deserted and their natural resources depleted. With this need for willing bodies to work, more immigrants came to the mountains, of all lineages hoping for a brighter future. The long-term effects on the land and the miner's health could never be replaced, let alone the large corporations treating the workers unfair with extraordinarily little pay and some even in debt to the company store.

Abandon Company Store in Virginia

Other natural resources that the outside world became aware of where the plants and herbs they could use for medications that run abundant in these mountains. Larger pharmaceutical companies would pay for locals to harvest ginseng, which would bring much needed income into their families. Knowing the ways of the land, numerous wise individuals would use the herbs provided in this unique fertile land to cure their own families long before larger corporations became aware of these hidden treasures. These remedies where passed down in families to those called Granny Women or Yarb Doctors.

As the world outside of these mountains moved along at what seemed lightning speed, the hillside was slower to develop, crawling along in our time capsule, so the difference in culture was very apparent when the War on Poverty started. The Appalachians was used as an example of what the world thought needed to be fixed. The world realized that it was very cut off from a certain standard of living, but instead of helping the situation it only inflicted more stereotypes of what people believed in the mountains. Again, the natives to the mountains were targeted with judgement, which only fueled the not trusting government or the outside world or so that is what some felt of the situation. Slowly, with programs put in place to help the poverty situation things have improved but still need a way to go.

Children had few toys / Photo by Wm. A. Barnhill, Gamaliel, Ark.
Creator(s): Barnhill, Wm. A., photographer
Date Created/Published: [between 1914 and 1917

Not everything can be measured by income or what you have of materialistic value because what the Appalachia did not have in monetary value, it greatly made up for in other areas. Family, community, natural resources, and spirit are all the things a person could never put a price tag on, and it is very abundantly running through these mountains. We have briefly touched on the history and the struggles that give us our flare for survival and life, now we are going to share some outstanding stories to show the undying spirit and mystical surroundings we have.

The women of these mountains have a hard life, most were married extremely young and had numerous children. To hear of a family of ten or eleven children was common. She cooked, cleaned, tended the house and garden, was the mother, doctor and sometimes all while having a husband who drank because of economic struggles and situations. These were women cut from a different cloth. They were strong and loving at the same time. A testament to this is a beautiful soul named Emma "Grandma" Gatewood. At the very spry age of sixty-seven she hiked the Appalachian Trail, which is not any easy task even for the more experienced hikers. She took on this endeavor in 1955 after escaping thirty

*Emma Rowena "Grandma" Gatewood, photo courtesy of Wikipedia*

years of abuse and raising eleven children. She is quoted for saying "if those men can do it, I can do it." She was the first woman to hike the trail but also the first person to do it three times.

One of the most famous features that bring visitors from all over is the Appalachian Trail. It covers from Georgia to Maine, and it is the world's longest foot-hiking path. The trail intertwines with all the areas in the Appalachian, it takes you to a place that most have lost track with. To complete the whole trail takes months. There have been books written and communities

*McAfee Knob on the Appalachian Trail*

formed around this life-changing experience. Whether you are hiking just for a day or on a life changing excursion this endeavor takes you to a simpler time, away from normal life to a place that life stands still, and you experience nature. It encompasses fourteen states and the most trails being Virginia. The Appalachian Trail Conservancy was established in 1925 to preserve and keep it a protected treasure.

Just as the Mountain ranges are majestic, they also hold secrets that are eons before our time. Even so far back to hold secrets for the dinosaurs. Remains were found of a dinosaur that is called the Appalachiosaurus. The remains were found in Alabama and are housed at the Tellus Science Museum. It was unearthed in June 1982 by geologists David King who discovered the juvenile. While this is not the only Dinosaur remains that have been found, in Saltville

*Appalachiosaurus, photo courtesy of Wikipedia*

VA there are numerous remains of a time long past that was drawn to the Salt deposits left from the seas. They were first brought to light by Benjamin Franklin, he understood that secrets from the past were hidden in the hills of the Appalachian, some of these even include the woolly mammoth.

. Other than trail hiking grandmas and dinosaurs, Appalachia holds many beautiful melodies that flow down through the hollers and hillsides, whether it is the buzzing of a new spring day, the wildlife that peaks out at night in wonder or the music that was brought over with the generations of immigrants. It is not uncommon for a kitchen or porch to be filled with the whole family and friends with an instrument of their choosing to create unique songs of struggles, daily life or professed love. Just as the people and culture were blended so were the beautiful sounds that bellowed down these mountains. Instruments and the unique style were handed down through different lineage such as the Scottish and Irish brought a sound and the Fiddle; German, French and Scandinavian countries brought the gift of yodeling and the dulcimer; African heritage contributions were the banjo and the rhythm and blues' soulful sounds. Numerous unique heartfelt tunes have come out of the homesteads of very gifted musicians that never left their front porch. Some instruments that would be handcrafted by clever musicians may include a washtub bass, spoons, and a washboard to add that extra Appalachian flare. Most families have fond memories surrounded by the beautiful songs of their culture.

*Appalachian Musician, photo courtesy Foxfire*

Some would say that as they heard the toe tapping music, it was hard not to move their body in some sort of way which led to the Appalachian's very own style of dancing, Flatfooting, bucking and even some tap elements. This unique style is a close resemblance to clogging, that mostly was self-taught. A custom of the hill people would be for someone with a large enough place to make a bargain with locals that wanted to dance. They would have crops that needed to be taken care of, such as corn needing to be shucked or beans that needed to be stringed. Negotiations would start of the terms that mostly stated once the crops were taken care of the volunteers could dance the night away in the space that was now provided with the tending to the crops. Most of the unique dance moves were either handed down or self-taught by watching others, which seems to fit right in with the normal learning style of the mountain people.

What goes hand and hand with the beautiful sounds of the mountains on a late summer's evening better than a sip of spirits or better known as the renowned moonshine, normally brewed by the

IMAGE COURTESY OF THE LIBRARY OF VIRGINIA

same family playing the instruments right beside you. The running theme as you have noticed is the defiance and untrusting nature of the Appalachian because of the hardships they encountered in their lifetimes and making their own mountain brew was no exception. Appalachia made a perfect backdrop for hiding and distributing the unlawful hooch. The roads in some locations were not accessible for local law enforcement, plus the locals knew short cuts through the mountains to deliver the homemade brew. As time went along runners were needed to deliver the bootleg brew but needed to be fast and unnoticed. They adapted cars that could run fast, were modified to carry corn liquor and looked normal. This is where the start of NASCAR came from.

As you have traveled with us into our home, in our history, we thought this section was important for you to see a brief glimpse into our past to understand where magic is cultivated. People still have a preconceived notion of what being an Appalachian means. Good or bad, we are a proud group that has come together in a melting pot to grow and flourish in harsh conditions. We have overcome numerous oppositions and that has made our magick strong and eclectic, just as our lineages are.

We are three strong Appalachian women who are stepping forward to say we are proud to be from these beautiful majestic ancient lands that our forebears came to make their lives better. We hope this gives you a better

understanding of how mystical we can all be as we harness our inter-Appalachian Witch.

# WHAT IS A GRANNY WOMAN?

Without you being from this area, you are probably wondering what a Granny woman could be, and the answer is simple, she was life.

Imagine at the incredibly early age of thirteen, fourteen or even fifteen being married and not just married but expected to raise children and God willing, a bunch of them. This is the start of a Granny Woman; young, innocent and a baby

Old woman smoking a pipe, Appalachia, USA, c1917. Photograph taken during Cecil Sharp's folk music collecting expedition: British musician Sharp (1859-1924) and his assistant Dr Maud Karpeles (1885-1976) collected folk songs from the mountain singers of the Appalachians (North Carolina, Tennessee, Virginia, West Virginia, and Kentucky), between 1916 and 1918. (Photo by EFD SS/Heritage Images/Getty Images)

taking care of babies. She was the head of the household while her husband went to work if they were lucky enough to have income, if not he could be tending to the farm, hunting or in the worst-case scenario intoxicated because of the surroundings and harsh conditions.

These young girls had to be smart, which most did not have formal education and strong, not in just childbirth but mentally to take care of all that was needed. As time went along, these young women learn from the land, what to give colicky babies, how to cure fevers, sicknesses and the list is endless. She started to assist with childbirth, she started to help with neighbors as they needed, and she became known as wise. These Granny women before us was the backbone of these mountains and if you do not believe me, think to yourself, who always made things better in your life?

Most of the time, your answer would be a grandmother or grandparent.

On these parcels of land cut off from the outside world, by now you understand the surroundings could be life threatening without proper understanding and knowledge, these Granny Women seem to have a knack for knowing what to do. This could be because she was handed down through her lineage the education, mostly by word of mouth. Some of the lineage had requirements, such as only one Granny Woman could hold the knowledge at onetime per family because they believed that if you give away the methods, they will no longer work. This superstition could cost a family hardship and lives, so you can see that this was painstakingly honored. Others believed the knowledge had to be handed down from female, to male and then back to female and so on (this is the Conner Sisters lineage). Each family and each holler were different but they all seem to have one thing in common, these beautifully strong wise women who did things a little different from each other but always ended with the same result, a healthy family, and friends.

Butter-making, Appalachia, USA, c1917. Photograph taken during Cecil Sharp's folk music collecting expedition: British musician Sharp (1859-1924) and his assistant Dr Maud Karpeles (1885-1976) collected folk songs from the mountain singers of the Appalachians (North Carolina, Tennessee, Virginia, West Virginia, and Kentucky), between 1916 and 1918. (Photo by EFD SS/Heritage Images/Getty Images)

Other than medicinal herbs and roots harvested, they also forged for food of roots, berries, nuts, and wild vegetables. In the mountains, if you had a Granny, you probably also remember getting up while the dew was still on the ground, picking berries and harvesting creasies from the fields, with no surprise what was your dinner for the night, greens, and berry cobbler. Without these memorable women, who knows where all the mountain people would be today.

It has been mentioned before that the heritage of these immigrants that settled the mountains and hillsides was not that of a trusting nature. With the hardships they faced, who could blame them. This untrusting nature was not just that of local authority or government it also was of healthcare. Most of us from the mountains have had horror stories told to us in the form of what happened to someone when they went to the doctor or the dentist. Still to this day, some of us suffer from what they refer to as "White Coat Syndrome," which is the fear of doctors and dentist, which could lead to high blood pressure and even panic attacks when they visit their doctor. Most people were barely making ends meet with financial hardships, so your health was put on the back burner a lot of times.

This was important in the way of the Granny Woman because she was a familiar face, one most trusted because she was one of their own and keeping her family in good health. Most of the time, she charged very little compared to a doctor. If she charged anything, she mostly worked out of her good nature. It was not unheard of for a Granny woman to just get a meal in appreciation or even something they would barter with, such as livestock or food. Her services that were much needed were her abilities to assist in childbirth. She would travel near and far, normally staying with the mother while she was in labor. She made for a smooth delivery all the while tending to the normal house of the expectant mother. It is not unheard of for the Granny to have a meal cooked for the mother after she delivered.

Being a midwife, tending to the dead and curing the sick were normal things a Granny woman did because she had generations of knowledge in her from numerous cultures including but not limited to, Native American, European, and African. This is where the term Folk healing and root work come into play. The most unusual is that a lot of these women were God fearing all the while enchanting charms, making potions and healing. The community openly embraced her and her conjuring ways. In these mountains it was believed they are God given gifts that are used and not addressed. Numerous times it has been brought to attention that you did not call yourself anything other than a Granny woman or healers even if you were conjuring up what needed to help. Putting a label on it would deter who needed the help, it is unknown if this was how the granny woman and culture thought of it, or if it was just subconsciously not spoken about. Either way she was revered as a wise, lifesaving, enchanted being.

This is where magick and the knowledge crossed paths. Her knowledge was well accepted but so was her enchanted ways. She would do unique rituals to make sure that her patient was well taken care of, for example her pregnant expectant mothers. It was a normal custom for her to show up with the hat of the father of the unborn baby and an axe. The hat was put on the mother to be a way of transferring the strength and resilience of the father during childbirth and the axe was put under the bed to cut the pain of labor. Of course, she also had numerous things she added to her workings, but these are a couple stand out practices.

Some stories have been passed down that Grannies were also referred to as "walkers" because in rare cases of the woman walking at night, she could not use a mule or horse for transportation because of risk in the animal stepping in a hole, so she walked. As these Grannies visited, whether on the back of a horse or mule or by walking, childbirth is what they were known for but her other gifts were just as important, such as talking the fire out of a burn, the ability to stop bleeding, curing thrush or wart removing.

Burning was important at this time in our history, most of your lively hood came from a fire, this is how you cooked and heated your home. Burns happened very frequently and could

Title: Interior of mountain farmhouse, Appalachian Mountains near Marshall, North Carolina Creator(s): Mydans, Carl, photographer
Related Names: United States. Resettlement Administration.
Date Created/Published: 1936 Mar

change a person's ability to provide for themselves, which was crucial. The granny woman normally had a cob pipe or dipped snuff or always had some sort of tobacco products on her, and this is why. She would take the dip or tobacco with spit and apply it to numerous skin inflammations and one use of her pipe was to blow the smoke on burns. She would speak and breathe on the burn, of course everyone was different, but the same constant act was to "talk" the burn out with your breath with or without the smoke and use hand movements over it.

Of course, Grannies always had some sort of tinctures, herbs or workings cooked up. People would either call on her or would visit her. They would look to her for advice and for guidance, and sometimes this would lead into divination, but of course it was called the gift of sight or dreams. Sometimes she would read tea leaves, coffee grounds, palms, bones, playing cards or just tell you what she was led to see. You can see why she was very respected and revered in our Appalachian culture.

Passing down the information from one Granny to another could be different just as the teachings in each family were. There are some that only passed their teaching to females and only when she was still able to bare children because they believed that a woman's power was the strongest on her cycle, so that is when she was taught the healing ways of the granny before her. Some would pass these doctoring to males and some would share their gifts with who they saw the spark that makes a granny woman great, their giving and healing nature.

We have mentioned before that people from the outside of these mountains have overlooked the contribution of African culture inside these beautiful hillsides, so we want to honor that by including them in the granny woman culture. Of course, they were among us in the Appalachian but also in the plantation regions also. African Granny Women were wise women that did the same in the mountains alongside of their immigrant neighbors. These strong women were honored on plantations throughout the south and helped with numerous babies being born to white and African families.

The running theme we have touched on before is the struggles, no matter what the nationality or your place of origin, healing was needed in these mountains to survive. As time has passed, society has tried to push the midwives and granny woman to be looked at as an obsolete item of the past. One of the ways they have done this is by numerous aspects, one being the need for proper training in facilities, deeming the traditions backwoods or witchcraft and one that seems to work very well on people in societies, your social standing. It was at one time thought of that the gentile woman didn't have to go through the pain as much as the poorer "sturdy breed." So, anyone who was mid class or upper class of course would not want to use an outdated granny woman but one that was normally a male white doctor. Some poorer standing families did find their ways to hospitals, because they wanted to get the same treatment as higher society, so much more than a granny woman could provide they thought, only to be able to be used in more clinical teachings by students rather than the proclaimed doctors so the students could learn and study.

*Three mountain women spinning yarn, 1939. The healers have traditionally served mountain communities. TENNESSEE STATE LIBRARY AND ARCHIVES*

This technique was used to rid the world of old outdated teachings such as the granny woman but what society didn't realize is that she is so much more than what they could see. The Grannies of these beautiful powerful mountains has a direct line to the greater good and what is needed for a flourishing lineage to withstand generations with pride and dignity.

So, the age-old question is presented, is it the knowledge that she held close to her or the magick in herself that helped numerous ailments, births and easing of deaths in this historic mountainous region? Was she able to tap into older energies that flow and course through these mountains? The question is for yourself to answer, as far as the three  Granny Women descendants who have chosen to share their magick with you, they know the answer.

The three ladies that have come together to author this book are direct descendants from these strong blood lines that run through these mountains. They have spent their whole lives in these hillsides and hollers, learning the ways with amusement and gratitude.

They want to preserve the old ways and educate new generations about just how magickal they can be. They are a new breed of strong women that are stepping forward to embrace their past, to be a voice for the future with their education, strength, and determination to share Appalachian Granny Magick wisdom with all who need.

U

## ~CAUTION~
## WORD TO THE WISE

As you have seen in previous chapters, we take our practices very seriously because at one time or another it means survival. The strongest magick you will ever encounter is fueled by emotions, and these mountains run fluently on them. Emotions can give the smallest workings the biggest impact. As you choose to read the spells set forth by each practitioner, know that they bring their own style of magick, energy to the spells, and their true voice as they write about themselves and their spell work. You will also do that as you add your own energy to these workings. Be aware that the results of these conjurings are in your hands and your responsibility. Practice safely, if there is any fire or ingredients you are allergic to, please use your own discretion. The ladies do not take responsibility for any mishaps or negligence in anyone's practice but their own. Be aware that these spells are either handed down through the families of the practitioner or ones they have cultivated and worked themselves. These are spells that work for the ladies and will for you also, so be sure before you proceed that this is something you genuinely want in your life.

If so, all results are the responsibility of the practitioner in charge of their own outcomes.

We hope you enjoy these magical workings.

**Happy Conjuring.**

---

*Many people will tell you that occultism, witchcraft, and magic are dangerous.*

*So they are, so is crossing the road, but we shall not get far if we are afraid ever to attempt it.*

*~Doreen Valiente*

---

# ASHLEY CONNER

# ASHLEY'S MAGICK

My name is Ashley Conner, and I am an Appalachian Witch, raised on a farm secluded away from the hustle and bustle of city life. I stayed true to the Appalachian witches before me as I created my own form of magic out of necessity and availability, rooted with superstitions, old family folklore and a love and respect of nature and animals.

Magic in my beliefs is what you make of it. There are many forms of magick, some can be ritualistic which is extremely strict rules and guidelines. Some folks like that and that is their magickal way, but my form and special flavor of magick is somewhat detailed only because I want y'all to understand my thoughts and reasonings so that you too can create your own. That will be by far more powerful than any spell you read or mimic. I was told early on when writing spells for anyone other than myself to always keep one ingredient out that witches know to add at least one thing to make it their own. So, if something feels right to you, then go on and add or change it up!

In our neighborhood Appalachian magic was not considered magic at all it was considered healing because if you were to claim you were a witch that would be against God and bad. Being a healer, no one would think twice about running to get help from when doctors were days travel away and medical supplies were sparse.

Growing up, I was always interested in other cultures of witchcraft but didn't recognize what we did on the farm as divination or witchcraft was just something you did. It was hidden under the rouge of "this is how it is." For instance, growing a garden, I was taught certain rituals to follow to make the plants grow because it was bad luck if you did not follow the rules.

My family line had a far dose of realism but there was magic in our upbringing and being a child of the south, you do not question your elders, you just do, it was a form of respect to not question. It is fair to say traditions are being lost, often because pawpaw or maw-maws have past and now instead of asking the old folks how you do something you have infinite knowledge at your fingertips, which being your phone. If you were to search for an answer it would give the practical way of doing things or more so the socially acceptable way. It is fair to say the magic is taken out of the equation, for instance removing warts was a secret practice passed down in my family, it would be passed down and taught from a male to female, and female to male. If you weren't the single selected opposite sex, you didn't get the information. If you were to web search for the answer of how to remove warts it would direct, you to your local drug store for some cream. The words magic was not used on the farm unless it was working magic on some old jalopy of a car to get it running. Sooner or later, we realized the terminology behind the word and exactly what in meant and realized hell we have been doing this all our lives! We knew it was out of character, they never blinked an eye when we rented witchcraft books from the library growing up or bought tarot cards, Ouija boards, and always had an interest in the unknown. There is always a constant fear of looking dumb or just talking nonsense, so it was not until we had become adults and moved out that we asked our family what they knew of witches and witchcraft. The reply was "they weren't called witches they would have gotten tarred and beaten they were healers, and your grandmother was taught to remove warts" and that gave the answer to the question we feared so long of asking.

When looking at what others considered "witchcraft," we were doing that on the farm and thinking nothing of it but to clear up common misconceptions some may have, we were never ones to abuse, torture or "sacrifice" animals. We were far to kindhearted and poor for that. We just wanted to heal them because that meant we would see Betsy the cow the next day, also if you kept your animals healthy then that's either money in our pockets when we took them to the market or honestly at times food on our plate. That was never something us poor Appalachians could wrap our heads around because you will never witness people from my neck of the woods throwing anything away because that in our mind is just throwing a dollar out the window. My family was not rich but did not let on to anyone we were poor. Being Appalachian, you will notice we survived on our own and had trust issues to anyone with authority. I may or may not have had a line of family members that believed they could do anything on their own including making and running shine. When the car got marked by the police, they would leave it in the woods and drive a different one for deliveries. Some outlandish stories, I still scratch my head in disbelief, is they actually buried a car to stay out of trouble. As any Appalachian American knows the law and shine running do not really get along much anyway. We knew by all means necessary to work and do what was necessary to provide and care for the ones back at home. My granddaddy was that prime example. He was a jack of all trades on the farm anywhere from raising crops to curing his own meat after one of the livestock was slaughtered to caring for a calf when the mother rejected it. His main job to supply for the family would be blue collar work. One particular job, he was a factory worker much like me, but at his factory he made tires. His brother and son worked alongside of him. My granddaddy watched his brother die in that factory by a large tire falling off a trailer and crushing him. My granddaddy went right back to work at the same factory. Later his son lost his hand, my granddaddy scared of losing his job, urged his son to take a settlement. Then you guessed it he went right back to work at that same factory. He had to provide for his family, and to any normal person it would be horrific but to him those were just things that happen.

You notice a lot of stories about coal miners and that is also in my family line but the going theme is no matter what you showed up for work the next day, if you were physically able because that is the only way the rest of the family would eat. A true old school Appalachian motto is your thankful for what you have and even as bad as it gets you hope and pray for to have it better one day.

As far as magic, everyone has a different belief system with the rule of three when doing problematic spells. I can only tell you my belief, I am not here to persuade anyone either way. I personally do believe in karma, but I also believe the rule is for the comfort of non-practicing people and those who it feels right to them. I believe that if the spell is just or justified and righteous then no harm will come to the caster. If a casting is not on the righteous side, then the spell will not go through if you have a pure heart in the situation and your intentions were not malicious then nothing will happen. If you're a person who wants to cause issues because you just have the ability, then I believe it would come with a price. I have seen some who cast just out of jealousy and it caused the caster a steep price, sometimes being their sanity.

Lastly, always be smart not cocky when casting with any healing spell or ritual. Be sure to seek professional medical help along with your casting, with that being said, happy casting y'all

## ASHLEY'S WORKINGS

| | |
|---|---|
| 1. Glamour item enchantment | 38 |
| 2. Removal of past hurtful words or traumas | 40 |
| 3. Make them see spell | 42 |
| 4. Prosperity bath time spell | 43 |
| 5. Love spell | 45 |
| 6. Garden grow spell | 48 |
| 7. Pet healing spell | 50 |
| 8. Confidence spell | 54 |
| 9. Spirit communication spell | 56 |
| 10. Eggshell powder protection | 59 |
| 11. Spirit communication with someone you know | 61 |
| 12. Appalachian Animal divination | 64 |
| 13. Mental cleanse for spiritual work and psychic development | 67 |
| 14. Intuition satchel | 69 |
| 15. House cleanse for happy home | 71 |
| 16. Good luck jar | 73 |
| 17. Depression and Anxiety Spell | 74 |
| 18. Enchanted spell pen | 76 |
| 19. Raise or promotion spell | 78 |
| 20. Stop gossiping | 80 |
| 21. Block a person's achievements and opportunities | 81 |
| 22. Return lost item | 83 |
| 23. Manifestation box | 84 |
| 24. Troubles cord spell | 86 |
| 25. Remove negativity bath | 88 |
| 26. Banish blues and bring positivity | 90 |
| 27. Clothing for empowerment and cleanse | 92 |
| 28. Karma/enemy inconvenience spell | 94 |
| 29. Seduction satchel | 96 |
| 30. New home spell | 98 |
| 31. Catching Fish Spell | 100 |
| 32. Flea Market Haggling Spell | 102 |
| 33. Safe Travels Spell | 104 |

# GLAMOUR ITEM ENCHANTMENT

**Herbs needed:**

- Jezebel root
- Roses
- Rose quartz
- Red candle
- Cardamon
- Cinnamon
- All spice
- Garnet
- Lavender
- Catnip
- Lilac
- Black eyed peas
- Basil
- Cedar-wood
- Small cauldron or flame safe bowl

Directions: choose a piece of jewelry, a sexy pair of undergarments or anything you would wear or bring with you, you can even enchant your makeup or perfume for at the time you use or wear these items. You will feel the glamour and power coming from them. The best spells or items are humorously seen in plain sight yet hidden, from an unbeknownst muggle.

Have your items intended for glamour on your alter or near you when performing glamour spells to rejuvenate the existing power and essence.

Place herbs into cauldron or fire safe bowl and burn while chanting.

"Make them see what I want

Make the hear what I need

Make them feel the words I heed"

Chant as many times as you feel correct. Three is the usual but sometimes you are led by your intuition to do more. Be sure to do spells with an open heart and full conviction but remember never to wish to be any other kind of beauty other than your own. People will not see your true light inside of you but only the mask you choose to wear.

After the spell wear your items with pride and confidence.

# REMOVAL OF PAST HURTFUL WORDS OR TRAUMAS

**Things you will need:**

- White candle
- Epsom salt exfoliating body wash
- Rosemary
- Lavender
- Roses
- Chamomile
- Lemon balm
- Peppermint
- Coffee grounds
- Large bowl
- Paper
- Pen
- Tweezers
- Full length mirror

**Directions:**

Light your white candle, write words that put harm upon you or the traumatic experience you is to close the book on in slips of paper, slightly link the paper to sign your name, allow to dry, take your large bowl put your base of the exfoliating body wash into the bowl, add herbs and coffee grounds mix ingredients together and inhale the smells imagining the issue you want to be forgotten leaving you. Now gaze at yourself in the mirror in the candlelight imagining yourself as beautiful and strong. Imagine how you would have handled the situation knowing what you do now. You are rewriting your own history before you to never think of it again. Watch your responses in the mirror and after you are satisfied with the closure, take your slips of paper, and place them into the flame as the words burn you are releasing the hold they had on you.

The bath-time herb mixture you have mixed is to rub upon your skin and imagine you are removing the hurt and shedding the skin to reveal a stronger shiny you. Recite in your head as you enjoy the exfoliation.

"What was broken now is new
Tomorrow I won't even remember you
Take this pain make it power
Memory both mind and body I did scour."

As you rinse your spell off your body as down the drain visualize the negativity returning to the earth

# MAKE THEM SEE SPELL

**Things you will need:**

- A black candle
- A photo of the person or their name on a piece of paper

This spell is for ones who are involved with people who tell a lot of falsehoods and manipulation traps, yet you feel no one else can see the deception but you. While doing the spell be sure to have emotion and conviction as you watch the flame flicker and grow, allow it to put you in a trance. While chanting three times

"Make them see who you are

Make them understand you aren't a star

Though your silver tongue spun a web

Now is the time your influence is dead"

# PROSPERITY BATH TIME SPELL

**Things you will need:**

- Green bath bomb
- Green candle
- Allspice
- Basil
- Calendula

- Chamomile
- Cinnamon
- Clove
- Flax seed
- Epson salt

*If you do not want the possibility of clogging your pipes with herbs, be sure to use a silk treat bah found in the celebration section of stores. *

Many underestimates a good old-fashioned bath, but a bath is a luxurious way to make a large spell to emerge yourself in if done correctly. Remember spells areas elaborate as you want or make them, this spell is meant to be very relaxed, your energy should be calm, and water like in a dreamy comfortable daze.

Imagine situations where you would like to receive money, items, or achievement, visualize right down to the minute details of what clothes you would be wearing. Note if any distractions or negative thoughts float into your mind be sure to delete the negative thought and start the pleasant scenario over.

# LOVE SPELL

**Items Needed:**

- A small red candle
- Salt
- Ground Cinnamon
- Rose Quartz
- Cardamom
- Coffee grounds
- Black eyed peas
- Love herbs mixture
- Basil
- Piece of brown paper
- A red ribbon

Sprinkle the salt around you or the area you are to perform the spell. Take three deep breaths clear your mind and take a moment to connect with your body and your spirit guides/Gods Goddesses/ deities and magic runners. Next take the herbs and place them into a small heat safe cauldron or flame and heat safe place to burn them.

(* note if you are not a fire loving witch and prefer to keep the herbs with you you may mix the herbs into a satchel rather than burn them)

Hold the rose quartz in your hand and whisper to the stone what you seek, whether it be love of yourself, love amongst friends or a romantic suitor.

<u>NEVER</u> demand a specific person, for it will be emotional kidnapping and your love will never be true. And you will be making this person a barrier to the true love you deserve. To advert this, you are to ask for the love that is meant for you by the universe at this time.

Then place the stone near you while the ritual continues. Write on the brown paper what qualities you would like in this relationship you seek out, lick the paper to create a bond and the body's signature making the words you wrote true from your mouth. Take a moment to mediate and visualize what you wrote on the paper bringing life to the words you wrote.

Then when your paper is dry, use tweezers or metal tongs to hold the paper into the flame, as the paper burns imagine you are releasing your dreams, hopes and desires out into the universe to return to you!

Wrap the red ribbon around your wrist and tie a knot 3 times, (if you feel more comfortable making the ribbon a keychain or other item, feel free to do so, this is your magick do what feels right to you just be sure to tie 3 knots while visualizing what you want. It is simple known magic and a visual representation of what you seek and not to settle for less, to stay of course of what you are looking for and never settle for mere availability rather than what you deserve.

The stone is to be kept near you to clear the way and attract the love you seek.

# GARDEN GROW SPELL

## INGREDIENTS/ STONES YOU WILL NEED:

- Malachite
- Moss agate
- Moonstone
- Clear quartz
- A chicken egg

## DIRECTIONS

\*\*Place stones at the base of the plants if only a few plants or if a whole garden you may plant the stones at the corners of the garden plot. Much like a crystal grid\*\*

Under the full moon and in the moonlight sit quietly and silently in plot where the garden is meant to be, imagine the garden being fruitful and full right down to the color of the leaves.

When ready to plant whisper to each seed sweetly, how you would like for them to grow, place the whole chicken egg at the roots of a plant that is considered the center of your garden. Recite three times.

"As this egg lays beneath your mighty roots, may you take its offering for the future bounty for myself and my family" so mote it be.

Cover the egg with the plant and dirt. Each full moon brings life back into your spell by visualizing the crop and the abundance that will come from the garden.

# PET HEALING SPELL

## PET HEALING RITUAL

Animals are extremely near and dear to my heart. I believe, animals are the purest form of emotions and have souls of humans just limited due to their forms. My lineage did not kill animals for divination purposes. That was wasteful and ridiculous to people surviving on the income we had. Myself, being raised up had many pets, my best friends growing up were animals due to there being no other children on the farm. So, they meant more than just a "pet" to me. Another issue was taking animals to vets was financially frightening for country folks with meek means, not to mention at times the animal passing and a hearty bill and the animal no longer with us. So, our first line of defense was to try to treat it ourselves. I learned to use my intuition and listen to the animals. An example, I have a rabbit that is a senior, nothing had changed diet nor habitat, and one day I picked her up and randomly measured her jawbone to her shoulder. I realized she had a slight head tilt; this was unrecognizable unless I had intuitively checked her in this way. She is a black double maned lion head, so her fur compensates a lot. When I noticed the issue, it was late Friday night, and I had no vet until Monday. Her health declined over the weekend to a critical point to take her to an emergency room. The emergency room vet was not able to find an issue but sent home critical care medications and food mixture. I brought her home because the stress of being at the vet could have made her worse. So, I took on the challenge of syringe feeding her and medicating her until I could get her to her normal doctor that Monday.

** Notice I am a person of the craft, also sought out professional medical help as well as presumed my own practice to save her. Be smart not cocky with your craft! **

I took my little fur baby home, she at this point had glazed over eyes and would not move or get up. I held my little bunny against my body like a baby after syringe feeding her, and I proceeded to imagine her body as a container from her head to her tail and I scanned her body for any imperfections or what in my mind's eye looked like black dirt, in a container of what in my mind was a thick light honey. I imagined my hand above her was a magnet to the black dirt that moved it out of her body. Of course, my emotions were raw and my desperation to save her empowered the spell/ritual, nonetheless. She fully recovered, the doctors still do not know fully what happened to her that brought her back, but she is a happy senior still to this day fully recovered. The emergency doctor was even amazed and asked how I was able to bring her back from the state she was in.

If you are aware of reiki this is much like that, I am a reiki master and have been attuned but I fully believe in times of need you have the power to help when it is truest needed.

### INGREDIENTS

- Yourself and intention of healing
- Selenite wand

## DIRECTIONS

Have your pet in a calm atmosphere, preferably laying down, relaxed, (this also can be used on larger animals such as horses, goats, and cattle, so standing is acceptable). Pray to your higher power for protection and healing energy. Close your eyes and hold your hand above the pet about 3-5 inches however feels comfortable to you. Run your hand over the pet's body if you feel any difference in the aura/atmosphere visually examine it and take note but remember to focus on that area for healing. Imagine from above a light pouring from the top of your head and pushing this divine light of healing through your hands. Place your hands on the animal and imagine transferring the white light to them and imagine throughout the body washing away any gunk or dirt within the body and exiting the feet. Run the selenite wand over the animal's body but do not let the animal chew on it or put it in their mouths, it will affect the wand.

# CONFIDENCE SPELL

### Things you will need:

- Two pieces of Fabric the size of a deck of cards (felt is best) a durable fabric
- Needle and thread
- Acorn
- Basil
- Anise
- Peacock ore
- Rose quartz
- Rose petals
- Catnip
- Bay leaf
- Cedar
- Chamomile
- Black eyed peas
- Cinnamon
- Coves
- Coffee grounds
- Orange peel
- Pomegranate seeds
- Saffron

**Directions**

Lay the two pieces of fabric on top of each other as sew the sides but be sure to leave an opening to place inside the herbs and stones. As you sew the satchel imagine yourself confident with an endearing factor that even if you fumble words or completely fall upon your face the audience of one or many will only see it as a relatable that will achieve you the desire of the conversation. You will add the various things into the satchel concentrating and adding your energy with each one. And as you add the last ingredient whisper your desires into the opening of your bag and hold it into your hands envisioning again your goal for confidence. Finish sewing the opened end, then wear the bag when confidence is needed.

# SPIRIT COMMUNICATION SPELL

## (UNKNOWN) SPIRIT COMMUNICATION

For spirit communication you can go many ways depending on the workers strengths, living conditions, and concentration. Take heed that spirits do not have the same timeframe as the living, so if first attempt does not produce stellar results do not get discouraged.

### INGREDIENTS

- CBD oil (optional)
- Tobacco offering
- Rose petals
- Chamomile
- Lavender
- White candle
- Snowflake obsidian for protection

## DIRECTIONS

To speak with spirits in a crowded haunted location I use CBD oil when the living's energy is strong. For me, CBD oil makes me feel more relaxed so I am able to put myself in a trace state, I also focus on the flame of a candle to "zone out". Burn the herbs as an offering for positive interactions with the spirits.

The candle is also used for communication as well as a focal point for your trance state of mind. While staring into the flame your vision should start to blur out and become fuzzy. It takes practice for some, and others are a natural at it. Once you reach the state of mind you will notice people around you can be talking but the words are harder to hear and recognize. Imagine with your mind's eye standing up and walking around the room. What do you see? Is there anyone there that is not physically there? Or something that looks out of place? If a different person is there, then the physical people try engaging into a conversation. In my experience and how my gift works they do verbally speak to me, often they show me feelings and small movies from their memories. So be aware some are not social, and you may only just get a glimpse of them. Others will, after you notice them will speak or communicate through the candle. As in making the flame higher or lower or at times make the candle spark. After this communication comes to a close, always make sure you thank them for the interaction, but your ways must part and they are to not follow you home or continue communication past this sitting.

# EGGSHELL POWDER PROTECTION

Eggs are an underestimated ingredient and magical object. Eggs can be used for protection, regrowth, fertility, to remove negativity and even divination. Eggs have more uses than breakfast plates or a tasty cake. You can also use egg whites as a facial mask. The shells can be used for fertilizers for plants, in strainers to keep your sink from being clogged. To even add in dogs' food for healthy additives. So, it would only be fair to think it would be beneficial in the craft. An old wife's tale states throwing an egg on your roof can protect you from other witches!

### INGREDIENTS

- Mortar and pestle
- Egg shells
- Dehydrator or oven

## DIRECTIONS

Crack the egg and use the insides for whatever you choose. Then take the eggs shells and dehydrate them until they are crunchy and dry. Put the eggshell into the mortar and use the pestle to grind the contents up. As you crush the eggshells be in deep concentration putting your intentions in for protection. As in visualize any negative force stopping in its tracks. Pray to your higher power for protection whenever this powder is used. Ground the shells to the consistency of your liking, some prefer gritty, and some prefer powder. It is truly up to the conjuror and the intended use of the powder.

# SPIRIT COMMUNICATION WITH SOMEONE YOU KNOW

## COMMUNICATION WITH A PASSED LOVED ONE

Growing up when someone had passed, my sister would dream of them after, this was always a sign to us they were ok, and it reassured of life after their body has given up. This oddly for some is the hardest and at times it is easier to communicate with an unknown spirit than a known one. And usually, you will get personalized signs such as seeing their favorite at an odd time that stands out to you. Or smelling their scent out of nowhere or hearing their voices in an empty house. I always tell clients I cannot guarantee a message or conversation. Because sometimes just letting their presences be known is all they want. Take into consideration if we were able to contact our loved ones who passed constantly like spiritual phone. And to speak to them about any and everything in our lives, or what we should do or what happens next. Fortunately, and unfortunately that is not the case. We would lose our free will to make our own choices and never get off the phone to live our own life. Occasionally we need or would like to know if they are ok or receive guidance and this is where this spell comes in. Do not take it to heart if you are unable to get the full conversation you seek when you seek it. because sprits have a different sense of time than us so it may take a few attempts and trials to get communication.

## INGREDIENTS

- A photo of the person
- Lavender
- Hags taper/Mullins
- Snowflake obsidian (for protection)

## DIRECTIONS

Before bed place a small bit of lavender and hags taper under your pillow along with the snowflake obsidian. Take a photo of your loved one and hold it concentrating on times you spent with them and the memories you have had. Speak from your heart to them about the matters you need to speak with them about. Place the photo under your pillow. Follow this each night until you see them or feel their presence in your dreams. Dream work is the easiest for me when seeking guidance from past loved ones. Due to that is when your walls of the physical world are down and allow interactions.

# APPALACHIAN ANIMAL DIVINATION

In the Appalachians, we tend to use animal divination. Meaning as in when a problem weighs heavy and you for instance are driving and a bear was to cross your path, we would consider that a sign. If your spirit animal was a bear, then you can translate as in you need to take on the characteristics of a bear to resolve your issue. Or due to the fact of it is your spirit animal then it can be translated into that you are on the right path and the situation will resolve in your favor. Use your intuition in choosing which one feels correct. Here is my animal interpretation to help your foretelling needs.

### APPALACHIAN ANIMALS

- Opossum- resiliency, adaptation, good luck, fertility, abundance, could represent a person is overreacting.
- Mule- stubborn, work, diligent, carrying most weight of the situation.
- Squirrel- renewal, energy, speeding the situation up.
- Cow- motherhood, generosity, gentle giant, balance.

- Rabbit- good luck, new beginning, hope, fertility, communication of those who have passed.
- Chicken- prosperity, abundance, underestimated, resourceful.
- Bear-courage to evolve, ability to have an open mind, temper issues, trust instincts.
- Horse- freedom, confidence, competition, loyalty and trust.
- Deer- instinct, serenity, gentle, victim, and intuitive.
- Cardinal- loved one who passed is letting you know they are there. Unexpected change.
- Chicken hawk- cautious, vulnerable, and predator.
- Crow- manipulation, mischievous, bad luck, mystery, and freedom
- Cicadas- we would always know summer was coming to an end to hear them. Transformation, incubation. Transition.
- Pig- lazy, gluttony, unaware of fate, misunderstood.
- Bobcat- majestic, menacing, strength, and power.
- Mountain lion- protection, adaptation, self-confidence, a treacherous situation is ahead.

- Raccoon- childlike, resourceful, intuition, make plans and calculations. See the situation from a different angle.
- Groundhog- loyalty, community, generosity.
- Whooper will-independence, stay strong in your convictions.
- Coyote- manipulation, hidden answers.
- Goat- stubborn, playful, need to be resilient.
- Snake- fertility, bad omen, be aware of who you trust.
- Mouse- good luck, household of happiness, and stop obsessing.
- Bat- new beginnings, let go of the old.
- Owl- magic, underworld, rebuild, transformation.
- Fox- calculated, good luck, protection, playful, take a new approach to the matter, quick thinking.

# MENTAL CLEANSE FOR SPIRITUAL WORK AND PSYCHIC DEVELOPMENT

### RELAXATION/PSYCHIC DEVELOPMENT EXERCISE

To go into any spiritual experience without clearing your mind and cleansing yourself. Can cloud your judgment, spells and if you go into haunted locations with a negative outlook and mindset you will attract that type of experience and spirits. This helps build your intuition, because it is clearing your mind to receive messages and take guards down as well as working on seeing with your mind's eye intricate details.

### INGREDIENTS

- A white candle
- Lavender
- Crystal quartz

## DIRECTIONS

Light the candle, and breath in the smell of lavender, hold your crystal into your hands.

Close your eyes, take a deep breath in and slowly let the air out, do this three times, clear your mind by only imagining clear lukewarm sun treated water cleansing and clearing out and negative energy. Imagine it coming from the top of your head all the way to your toes returning to earth. Imagine the negative energy of dark debris.

Now I want you to imagine a black room, nothing in the room but you see a spotlight coming from the ceiling. And in this spotlight you are to notice a white fluffy feather. Imagine the feather in your mind as if you were to see it with your eyes open. Imagine it swaying softly left and right slowly, imagine each fiber of the feather swaying until it finally reaches the floor. Then you may open your eyes feeling refreshed and the weight of the world off your shoulders.

# INTUITION SATCHEL

I personally carry an intuition spell/satchel with me, I prefer satchels because they are discreet. You can always pass them off as an air freshener to anyone who would question why you would do spell work. A smart witch will always hide her magic in plain sight so it gets the energy it needs to keep the magic alive.

## INGREDIENTS

- Purple cloth (preferably piece of a purple shirt you have worn)
- Moonstone
- Chicory
- Quartz
- Peppermint
- Amethyst
- Rosemary
- Lavender
- Mullins/hags taper
- Mugwort
- Star anise
- Basil

## DIRECTIONS

If you have an old purple shirt, you have worn that would be best to use because it already has your energy on it. Cut the fabric/shirt into a square and sew three sides. Add the stones and ingredients into the square. Hold the bag in your hands and pray for protection, guidance, and truthful insight. Thank your spirit guides and then sew the satchel shut. Place the satchel under your pillow for 3 days to bond with it. Then carry it with you when extra help is needed. After a year of using be sure to burn the contents and thank it for its help. Then feel free to make a new one.

# HOUSE CLEANSE FOR HAPPY HOME

When your home seems more tense or more arguing occurs, be sure to use this spell. Every-time my mom, myself of my sister was upset about any situation whether it be a death or illness in the family or just plain having the blues. My mom would make us clean the house. She would never tell why but she would always ensure it would be better after. Magically speaking the energy flow is better when things are clean but also, certain cleaning products hold more than just a punch on dirt. Additives such as lemon grass and pine have magical uses. Lemon grass is an ingredient in van-van oil and is known for healing, protection, money, and cleansing.

## INGREDIENTS

- Murphy's oil or Pine-Sol (be careful of furry friends/pets because some are more sensitive)
- Rose quartz
- 4 Obsidian stones
- Bucket
- Mop

## DIRECTIONS

Pour floor cleaner into a bucket and dilute the mixture with water like normal. Then pray over your bucket to what deity or higher power you connect with. Recite

"As I wash the floors of this house, I also wash the negativity and chaos from myself and my family."

Recite three times and thank your higher power.

After the cleansing has concluded place a rose quartz in the heart of the house to bring peace and love into the home. Next take the obsidian stones and place them in each corner of the house to keep the negativity out.

# GOOD LUCK JAR

Everyone should do this spell because sometimes in life you just need luck on your side. In the Appalachians, a horseshoes hung right side up like a "u" was considered to bring good luck. But if you happen to be low on horseshoes then this jar will do the trick.

## INGREDIENTS

- Jar
- A penny you found right side up
- Clover
- Black eyed peas
- Ginger
- Cinnamon
- Lavender
- Basil
- Frankincense
- Acorn
- Wishbone
- Dandelion wishes
- Rice

## DIRECTIONS

Be sure to place it beside or over a doorway to generate energy and bring good luck into your home.

# DEPRESSION AND ANXIETY TEA AND CANDLE

If you have occasional blues, then this spell will brighten your day. But be sure to consult professional help if it persists or you have thoughts of harming yourself and or others.

## INGREDIENTS

Tea choices: chamomile, green, ginger root, or lavender tea

- White candle
- Basil
- Orange peel or oil
- Rosemary
- Lavender
- Bay leaves
- Rose pedals
- Pine needles
- Himalayan salt
- Obsidian stone
- Smokey quartz
- Peacock ore
- Teacup
- Flame safe small cauldron

## DIRECTIONS

This spell is to be done in the morning because you want a fresh start mentally. Have a cup of tea with one of the following main ingredients. Store bought I would trust the most because myself am not a tea maker. You will need one of the following depending on your taste and or preference. Chamomile, green tea, ginger root, or lavender. As you sit with the tea you will light your white candle.

Burn the following ingredients in the small flame safe cauldron, orange peel, lavender, basil, rosemary, bay leaves, rose petals, and pine needles. Place the Himalayan salt in a bowl on the table and imagine it filtering out all negativity and filtering in good energy. Place the quartz beside the candle on the left, place the obsidian beside the candle on the right and the peacock ore in front of you. Put yourself into a trance concentrating on the flame in front of you. Stir your tea counterclockwise three times to remove your negative feelings and anxiety. Then stir clockwise three times to bring positive thoughts and happiness. Drink the tea, focus on the flame, and imagine things that would bring happiness and feel the negative thoughts leaving and behind you. When the herbs have extinguished dump the ashes next to a walkway or road so the spell can continuously get energy. Keep the stones with you as a reminder.

# ENCHANTED SPELL PEN

You probably have noticed you have a preference in location you sit for spell work, you may have most likely noticed certain things out of habit makes you feel at ease in your personal space or magically speaking the energy just flows better. So why would your writing utensil be any different? Some spell workers use certain ink, certain wooden pens or myself, I purchase clear tubed pens and I do different versions for different genres of spells. In this version I will be making petition/spell pen for the less fuzzy happy spells. This pen can be used for protection, to speak with spirits or spells for inconveniences to the target.

## INGREDIENTS

- Clear tube pen that holds objects in a different container than ink
- Graveyard dirt
- Four black candles
- Salt
- Box

## DIRECTIONS

If collecting the graveyard dirt, yourself be sure to leave an offering, and be sure you make/had a relationship with the person who you took this from. If the grave makes you feel negative around the grave do not take from it.

To prep the graveyard dirt: Place the graveyard dirt in a small container. Then put salt in the box and place the graveyard dirt in its container in the salt for 3 days.

Light the black candles with you and the pen in the center. Place the dirt inside the pen container. And recite these words, while imagining you charging your energy into the pen.

"With these words I recite,

Requesting for justice when I write

Keep me protected from the ill will,

With ink I write let my truth be seen still"

Recite three times each time with your heart and intention into it.

Ending the spell with so mote it be.

# RAISE OR PROMOTION SPELL

## GETTING A RAISE/ RECOGNITION

Sometimes in your profession you feel overlooked and not appreciated. This spell is to achieve recognition. Be sure to cleanse your mind and body so you do not bring in negativity and receive recognition for the wrong reasons.

### INGREDIENTS

- Moon water
- rainwater
- Green candle
- cinnamon
- Basil
- ginger
- Acorn
- rice
- glitter
- Penny
- catnip
- Jarold
- key no longer used
- White

## DIRECTIONS

Light the green candle and let it burn as you follow the next steps. Place all items except the acorn, candle, and key into the jar, next speak inside the jar what you want and hope for then put the lid on the jar. Shake the jar to activate the spell. Place the key on top of the jar and place the jar on a windowsill so that the moon can charge it. Place the acorn in your wallet or wherever you keep your money or check card. Each day for 3 days, shake the jar. This is bringing energy into your spell and after 3 months' time pour the contents of the jar beside a walnut tree and thank the universe. Keep the key to unlock future opportunities.

# **STOP GOSSIPING**

Most people have at least one person who gossips, lies, and puts ill will toward others, them, or someone they love. This spell is to make them stop.

## INGREDIENTS

- A photo of them or draw a face and put their name on the forehead.
- Thread and needle
- Black candle

## DIRECTIONS

Take the photo and sew the mouth shut, place the photo in your right shoe, for three days wear these shoes because the interactions of their drama are beneath you. After three days burn the photo but keep the ashes and flush them down the toilet.

# BLOCK A PERSON'S ACHIEVEMENTS AND OPPORTUNITIES

This is the spell to stop someone's achievements and opportunities. For a goal-oriented person this is the ultimate punishment. If there is a person who tries to be in competition whether it be for a job, partner, or just in general who is just not an overall good person then this spell would be for you to cast.

** do not cast this spell just because you are in a bad frame of mind about this person. Be sure to weight the reasons why you are trying to stop this person before casting. **

### INGREDIENTS

- A rock
- Photo or representation of the target (this can be their name on a piece of paper)
- Know where a tree where a woodpecker has made a hole or a sappy hole in a tree.

## DIRECTIONS

Take the photo or representation and think of all the wrong this person has done. Then place the photo on the floor and place the rock over the photo face down. As you are covering the photo imagine opportunities over passing them, and then being overlooked and never quite making the cut. Leave the rock on the photo undisturbed for 3 days. Then crush the representation into a small, crinkled ball and place it inside the tree hole that is sappy to slow them or a woodpecker hole to cause chaos.

# RETURN LOST ITEM

### RETURN TO ME LOST ITEMS SPELL

When you have misplaced an item either it was not meant to be yours or it is not meant to be used at this time. But sometimes a simple lost item is just that an item you need to call home.

### DIRECTIONS

Close your eyes, take a deep breath, imagine your item and the purpose for needing it. Then in your own honest words simply ask for your spirit guides to open your eyes to its where a-bouts. If you saw a glimpse of where it could be in your mind's eye, then thank your guides and investigate the location. If no imagery came through, then ask if possible, the item is returned or what is meant to be yours be brought back. Leave an offering of tobacco or any natural herbs from your land for thanks for their help. Usually, the item will return to me within 24 hours. Be sure to establish a relationship with your spirit guides as in thanking them and showing your appreciation for their guidance.

# MANIFESTATION BOX

A manifestation box is to achieve your goals and set your heart's desire. It puts them out into the universe so that you attract what you want much like the law of attraction.

## INGREDIENTS

- Peppermint
- Himalayan salt
- Basil
- Quartz
- Cinnamon
- Carnelian stone
- Rosemary
- Peacock ore stone
- Cloves
- Written paper of goals or photos
- Chamomile
- A box

## DIRECTIONS

Feel free to make your own box as decorated or casual as you want. Make it you! Place the herbs and stones into the box let this ferment for three days' time. Take slips of paper and write what you want, even photos of your goals. Envision yourself with these goals accomplished and achieved, put your spit on each one (this is like your signature). Place the paper in the box. At least once a week open the box and reflect again on your desires. Place your hand on top of the box and visualize the magic stirring inside. When your desires have been met and accomplished be sure to burn the slip of paper and thank the universe for it.

# TROUBLES CORD SPELL

### TROUBLES LADDER/KNOTS

When life gets overwhelming, and you feel stuck in situations. Such as for example a work atmosphere and you are unable to express, your true feelings this spell traps your troubles and keeps the peace. The issues may not necessarily be resolved but it takes the feelings from you and allows you to let it go and see the situation from a judgement point without heated feelings.

### INGREDIENTS

- Fodder twine or store-bought juke cord

### DIRECTIONS

Take the twine or cord and wrap it around your stomach area three times. This is to collect your energy and connect to your solar plexus chakra which is responsible for helping you feel in control in your life. When the cord is wrapped around you pray for any troubles you knot into this cord that is finds a solution and releases you from the pressure of the situation. Cut the cord.

Take the cord and fold it in half, then make a knot to leave a loop to hand your troubles up mentally and literally when you're done. Sit in a quiet non disturbing place and meditate on your woes and troubles and as they come to you tie a knot in your string. This is trapping it out of your mind. Use your judgement/intuition on how many knots you need to make.

When you have released yourself from the day's session hand the cord and pray that your higher power helps the situation and relieves the pressure it has on you.

# REMOVE NEGATIVITY BATH

When you feel overwhelmed and feel down it is time to cleanse yourself of negative energy.

## INGREDIENTS

- Moon water
- Rosemary
- Lavender
- Eucalyptus
- Epsom salt
- Handkerchief
- White candle

## DIRECTIONS:

Light the white candle, draw yourself a bath and put the Epsom salt and the moon water into your bath. Place the remaining herbs into a handkerchief, tie a knot three times then put the handkerchief in the bath. Imagine this being a magical caldron with only the last ingredient being yourself. Lay into the bath and imagine the soak taking all the negativity off. When you feel lighter and efficiently spiritually cleansed imagine as you drain the water you are also draining the sludge of what was weighing on you down the drain as well. Your next step is to check your aura, which is closing your eyes and holding your hands a few inches above your body and starting at the top of your head and slowly moving to the bottom of your feet. If you feel a difference in the atmosphere, then there may be some sludge still on your aura. When checking your aura different individuals feel different things. Because everyone is unique of course and this is your own magic. But just to give you an idea, some feel heat, some feel electricity, some even feel pressure. That simply means the energy flow has issues in that area. The next process if an aura complication occurred is to imagine a white light from your hand dusting the negativity away. (I normally imagine the negativity as a muddy surface and the light from my hand a power washer that takes it away and returns to the earth.)

# BANISH BLUES AND BRING POSITIVITY

Ever heard of the Hank Williams or Patsy Cline song "Walking after Midnight" this spell is like the theme song to it.

## ITEMS NEEDED

- Waking shoes
- Favorite grounding stone
- Favorite music

## DIRECTIONS

**Be sure to be safe, aware of cars and aware of your surroundings**

Put on your favorite grounding stone in your pocket, put on your comfortable walking shoes and select your favorite music to listen to. And in the moonlight while you are walking away from your beginning location think of all the situations you want to release this is meant to take the problems from you and ground you. Feel the power of the moon energizes and purify you. Walk as long as you feel able and necessary. When you feel you have confessed your blues to the moon turn around and begin walking toward your starting point. Think of only positive things you want to bring to you and positive situations.

** This is also a great grounding technique for ghost hunters or anyone who feels they have energy on them that may not be theirs. It's a releasing ceremony. **

# CLOTHING FOR EMPOWERMENT AND CLEANSE

When a witch needs to draw energy in an inconspicuous way that the causal non-casting wouldn't recognize as abnormal. Color magick is an effortless way for something unnoticeable and small to pack a magical punch. For instance, wearing the color black stands for authority and protection, orange is confidence, yellow is happiness, brown stability, blue is loyalty, purple represents royalty and psychic development lastly of course white is universal and purity.

### INGREDIENTS

- A box
- Salt
- Quartz
- Lavender scented laundry detergent

## DIRECTIONS

Each day you pick up the energy around you, so be sure to remove that unwanted energy from your clothes. I am a person whose allergies cannot take sage so I place a quartz crystal in the bottom of the washer. And use the lavender scented laundry detergent, depending on the clothes color if you would rather use a small bit of real lavender or essential oil that is just as good but lavender scented detergent is more clothing friendly and simplest. After the clothes cycle has finished collect your stone and let it dry. Then place your stone in a box of sale to purify it for three days. Then charge your stone by moon light and it's really for be next task!

# KARMA/ENEMY INCONVENIENCE SPELL

I am one that would wish minor inconveniences on someone who has what I felt intentionally done me wrong. So, I made a spell for it, and it works quite well. I once lived near someone who had done wrong to me and to show my spell workin. I left my family cookout and at the end of my driveway I saw my spells target driving down the road and out of nowhere, in the middle of the day. A deer ran out of nowhere at this person's car and ran off unharmed. The car was dented, and this happened right in front of me. (**BE SURE to only cause justice for the wrongdoing NOT just to be petty. Because if not rightfully deserved this will come back on you. **)

## INGREDIENTS

- photo of target or something to represent them
- Slip of paper explaining how they wronged you
- Garlic
- blackberry root

- Coconut
- lime or lemon
- Blueberry
- chicory
- Chili powder
- nettle
- A pot
- stove
- Boiling water

**DIRECTIONS**

Place the pot with the water on the stove make the water come to a boil, then place all ingredients except the photo/representation of the person and the paper stating the wrongdoing.

Now let the items boil and cause a pot of inconvenience, place the target into the hot water then the justification paper. Let it concoction marinate and boil for however long feels right to you. Then drain the water and pour it near a path be it a road or walkway that receives a lot of energy. And bury the remaining contents opposite to you homes entrance to insure it is behind you yet not forgotten.

# SEDUCTION SATCHEL

Sometimes you need a little something extra to be seductive in situations weather to be that sex kitten that slows down the room and all heads turn or being suggestive on a date.

## INGREDIENTS

- Cinnamon
- red rose petals
- Red candle
- cardamom
- Ginger
- paper
- Red lip stick
- magnet
- Raccoon penis bone
- satchel/red

## DIRECTIONS

You are to place everything except the red lipstick and paper into the small satchel. Whisper into the bag what you want the herbs to do to give you the outcome your heart desires. Take a piece of paper and write how you want others to perceive you. Put the red lipstick on and seal the request with a kiss. Fold the paper towards you, hold the candles unlit into your hands and close your eyes and imagine your most sexist energy coming from your body infusing into the candle for as long as you feel right. Place the candle in a heat and flame safe container/area and light the candle. Let it burn a moment and feel the energy radiate into the room. When it feels right take your paper and burn it. Place the lit paper in a flame safe open container and let it burn out because you are to collect the ashes and put them into your satchel. Continue to burn the candle each night for 3 nights. Carry the satchel with you or in close proximity until you have absorbed the essence of the spell. Listen to your intuition as to how long to carry the satchel.

# NEW HOME SPELL

Of course, this spell is to bring the correct house to you p. Not necessarily getting you to win the publisher's clearing house. This spell is meant to draw energy you need into finding a new home meant for you.

## INGREDIENTS

- Catnip
- peacock ore
- Pomegranate
- brick shavings/powder
- Wish bone
- turtle shell
- Basil
- lavender
- Coffee
- your spit
- Knight of wands tarot card
- Ten of cups tarot card

## DIRECTIONS

Take all ingredients except the tarot cards and put them into the turtle shell. Place the turtle shell on top of the two cards. Let this sit near a window under the full moon. Sit and visualize what you would like as a new home, even down to the location and neighborhood. Imagine the back yard and front yard, visualize your dream home. And sit with the moon envisioning this desire.

Then thank all that is assisting in this home that is to be in your path. In the morning bury all but the two tarot cards. If you do not have a yard to do so you may bury this under a potted plant and that will do just fine.

# CATCHING FISH SPELL

When you see a skilled fisherman it looks like pure magic, so of course why wouldn't there be a spell for it?

**INGREDIENTS**

- A dead cricket
- Four leaf clover
- Hag's stone
- A penny found heads up. (Or one you have on hand)
- Fishing hat
- Deer antler or a deer antler tip
- Dried pineapple piece

**DIRECTIONS**

This needs to be done for the best results on a full moon, morning, or evening. Note if cows are laying down you're not going to catch anything. So be aware of nature and the signs of a good fishing day. Place and keep in your tackle box, a four-leaf clover, hag stone, a dead cricket (usually able to get this from the tackle shop) and a piece of dried pineapple.

Next take a hat you wear and put the "Fehu" rune symbol on the tag or somewhere inside with a black magic marker. On the way to the fishing hole, place a deer antler under your seat and leave it there. If you have a keychain of a deer antler tip that is even better. As you reach the water toss a penny, preferably one you found heads up. But one you obtained will do as payment and offering. (I keep pennies as offerings to anything I take from nature. Make sure you give back for everything you take and make sure it is eco-friendly) As you sit with your line in the water, clear your mind and imagine releasing any tension or stress to the earth. Next as you feel relaxed imagine catching a fish visualize as much detail as you can of a fish choosing your line. Note to never think negativity while fishing. Always think of everything positively because mind set is everything. After you are done fishing for the time. Thank the waters either that be aloud or a moment of goodbye in your mind, be sure to show appreciation for the experience to nature.

# FLEA MARKET/YARD SALE HAGGLING SPELL

If you have ever walked the aisles of the flea market to find a dusty treasure and seek the trill of a negotiation or deal in your favor, then this is the spell you need.

### INGREDIENTS

- Coin purse
- Eucalyptus
- Cinnamon
- All spice
- Penny
- Saffron
- Basil
- Piece if tin
- Mint
- Lock of your hair
- Two gold rings
- Two rubber bands
- Green tourmaline
- Malachite

## DIRECTIONS

Take your small coin purse and place the cinnamon, penny, basil, mint, eucalyptus, all spice, saffron, green tourmaline stone, malachite, and the piece of tin. Next take the lock of your hair and place a rubber band on one end. Then braid the hair and secure it with the other rubber band at the end. Then place it in your coin purse as well. Carry this with you when you plan to haggle. Take the two gold rings and place them on your left hand, on your index finger and your pinky.

# SAFE TRAVELS SPELL

This spell is to ensure you have the magical aspect of safety on your side. I have made these little jars and placed them in each car I have ridden in and own.

## INGREDIENTS

- Mini jars
- Mini funnel
- Garlic
- Black ribbon
- Salt

- Black candle
- Lavender
- Parsley
- Oregano
- Rosemary

## DIRECTIONS

A small jar from the dollar tree or a craft store works the best. Be sure to get a funnel to fill your jars but you can also roll paper to better guide your herbs in if a funnel is not available. Light the black candle. Then place all the herbs into the bottle cork the bottle then tie the black ribbon around the jar neck three times. Then seal the top with black wax. Place the jars in your luggage, under seats of your car or even in motorcycle side bag.

# MISTY CONNER

# MISTY'S MAGICK

Every person's magick is unique just like a fingerprint or a signature. Your magick is your spiritual signature you leave for the other side, or this is how I like to think of it.

I am Misty Conner, born and raised on a small farm in the Appalachian Mountains with my sister. I have lived all my life in the confines of these magical mountains and there is a pride that is handed down through generations that also comes with that. I am sure most have heard of the haunting tales or the superstitions that have echoed through these hollers about all the creatures, lore and legends. I could say they were not true to ease some, but that would be a discredit to all that have walked these haunted lands before us, because they are true. Handed down by word of mouth as cautionary tales and words of wisdom because everyone knows some of the most outlandish stories are rooted in truth, and these are no different. This is also what gives an Appalachian a different view of spooks, haints and superstitions, because we have lived it our whole lives. It comes seconds nature to us, part of us and magick is just a small piece of the big puzzle that makes up an Appalachian Witch or Granny Magick as some would call it.

This is how Appalachian Magick works in my eyes and on my path. In these mountains there was a collection of people that survived and blended their various gifts together to make sure their loved ones, crops and themselves could live to see another day. This is a collection of gifts, intuition, and lineage that combines to make one of the most captivating forms of spell casting. Each holler could have a different variation of how to achieve their goals, whether it be to make their crops grow, heal ailing children, or just conjure peace between neighbors, each had something a little different, a little twist to the puzzle. Each family conjuring a little different is also what makes Appalachian Magick different than the rest. There is no official set of rules, no one went to classes to achieve these abilities, it was handed down through each generation.

My sister, Ashley and I's lineage include what people consider in the mountains a wart witch, the conjurer is able to pull unwanted things from the body, in this case warts. The unique part is it had to be handed down from male to female, or female to male. My father remembers the night he accompanied his sister to his uncles. The uncle was able to remove these unwanted warts by simply "talking" them away, and my father was witness to this. After they left on the way home, my father as a young man watched in amazement as his sisters' warts vanished.

The will of the people in these mountains were surpassed by none. That will is what many of our ancestors had to rely on when they faced hardships, such as walking days to reach a coal mine so they could provide for their family, like our great grandfather did.

It was in everyday life, the ability to adapt and survive. What we call magick now was a survival technique used by our ancestors. Such as our great grandmother, which we lovingly called Granny; she was able to cure many things with snuff and her spit. Now I know by conventional means, spit would not be your choice of medication, but she would combine it with snuff, which she dipped in her lower lip, to apply to numerous things such as bee stings or ailments of the skin. How she knew to do this was her having to be the mother, doctor, and provider for her family. These are the little things that combined to make our rich history. Was it the tobacco in the snuff that helped the sting or was it her intent in her spit that cured her loved ones. That is the true question of magick, isn't it not?

As you develop in this world so does your magical side. You will find that when you start down this path you will be pulled to certain aspects that later, no longer serve you but the beauty of it is, as you travel your path you take tid-bits of all aspects to make your special blend of manifestation. This is where uniqueness comes in, there is no one like you in this magickal world.

I have found that on my path I have been drawn to numerous forms of root and folk magick which is strong within our bloodlines. Many settlers were immigrants, Indigenous and some just wanting to be free of oppression that lived in harmony in these beautifully captivating mountains. In my spells, you will find simple ways to manifest what you will. The hardships of the mountains sometimes left the practitioner with only simple items to cast from, and you will see these elements come forward in my practice.

As you develop down your path, make sure you explore what calls to your soul or just feels right, most of the time, you will find you are being pulled that way because it is a path that was always destined for you. It could mean that your ancestors before you walked a slightly different path and you can feel that pull in this life, just as each holler in the Appalachians conjured just a little different, every practitioner does too. Do not be afraid to let your intuition guide you.

I hope you enjoy these spells just as I have enjoyed cultivating them for you.

# MISTY'S CONJURINGS

1. Apple Break up spell — 112
2. An Apple peel Spell To tell who your betrothed is — 116
3. Be Gone Powder — 118
4. A Charm for Female Energy — 121
5. Appalachian way of telling the sex of an unborn baby — 124
6. Come to Me oil — 125
7. Cord Cutting Spell — 127
8. How to get rid of unwanted visitors with ill intent — 130
9. Honey Jar — 134
10. How to Bless salt, oil, and water — 136
11. How to do a Petition — 139
12. How to make a person yours until their ends — 142
13. How to remove a curse — 144
14. How to tell if you have a Curse on you — 150
15. How to tell if a Spell has backfired or failed — 152
16. Knot Magick — 158
17. Mirror Wear and Repeal spell — 160
18. Money, Money, Money Oil — 162
19. What is ok to use in Spell work? — 164
20. Stop Male Sexual Desires (infidelity stopper) — 167
21. Prosperity Jar — 171
22. To Ward and Protect your property — 173
23. Black Protection Salt — 177
24. Road Opener working — 179
25. Safe Travel Conjure — 181
26. Soulful Cleansing Bath — 185
27. To get rid of bad energy in your house — 188
28. How to hide someone from spell work — 190
29. Truth Spell — 193
30. Your enemy's demise — 198
31. To call back something you lost Conjuring — 201
32. Full Moon Manifestation Working — 203
33. Stress reliever — 205

# APPLE BREAK UP SPELL

Warning to all that take on this spell, if you practice with the intent of Karma, do understand that if you are forcing any will you have to reckon with your belief system.

In the mountains, the law of the land is as in the Bible "an eye for an eye" still to this day whether you are a regular person or one that dabbles in conjuring, most believe this rule but not all. So, to each their own. A good example of this is the Hatfields and McCoys, feuds can last a long time and people tend to look for options. Godly or not.

To defend yourself, your loved ones or to counter any other persons' workings against them is very acceptable to cunning folk in these mountains, also. If you find yourself in a position where you need this spell, then here is all you need. Do understand that for a relationship to completely end, it is meant to be decided by the two parties and fate BUT if that relationship is not based on a strong structure or good intent, this spell can help to pull the two apart.

## INGREDIENTS

- An Apple
- A knife
- Vinegar or lemon juice
- A picture of both parties, separate pictures
- Nails, pins, anything sharp or rusty
- Twine or something to tie the apple together
- Optional- any items that are small of the couples that can fit in the Apple, ex. hair, nail trimmings, signature.

## DIRECTIONS

Take your apple and cut it in two pieces. As you do make one side be for the one party in the relationship, and the other for the other party. If you have personal items place them on the freshly cut side of the apple, if not place the picture of the one party in the relationship FACE DOWN into the freshly cut apple. Do that also for the other side of the apple for the other party. The concept is to never let them see eye to eye, they will have their backs to each other and be looking elsewhere.

The whole time you are doing these workings think of the outcome you want, with the two waves of the apple with their pictures placed face down into the Apple, the next step is to spur the relationship, pour the vinegar or lemon juice over the apple, make sure to cover both parties. There are no specific words to this spell, it is all about intent and a person who uses this with scorn in their heart has more power and intent than words can explain. So, none is needed, you will know what to think and say as you do your work to make it more of your own. Now put the two halves together but as you do take the pins, nails, or any sharp items you collected and puncture them through the apple, with each pin you put in the Apple think of the reason you want this couple apart. When you are done, (make sure to at least put in three sharp items or a multiple of three) take your twine and wrap the apple together, every time you pass the apple completely make a knot, and again think of your outcome, this is knot magick. Do this at least three times.

No place this apple in a dark place no one can see it and think it of no more, as the apple rots so will the relationship.

\*For an extra kick of intent, if you want to use any fluids of your own, such as urine or spit that can also be used in this spell.

# AN APPLE PEEL SPELL TO TELL WHO YOUR BETROTHED IS

In the mountains, apples are a delicacy. I remember taking my granddaddy when he was older to an orchard so he could get handpicked apples in a big brown poke. He looked like a kid in a candy store. So, you can see where this would be a key ingredient in numerous spells. They were easy to come by and easy to work with. Plus, an apple is the definition of knowledge which goes all the way back to Eve in the Garden. and let's not forget about the fertility and abundance side of an apple.

I am covering two completely different spells that use apples. The first is how to tell your Betrothed, the one you're meant to be with, your soul mate.

### INGREDIENTS

- Red apple
- Knife for peeling the apple
- Come to me oil (optional)

## DIRECTIONS

Pick yourself an apple to which you are drawn. I am a big believer in your use what is meant for you. Whether it is walking in your yard, picking a ripe apple you have planted and grown yourself or just going to your local Kroger's and picking the best one you feel, both are meant if they find their way to you. Next, wash the apple, as you cleanse it, think of the attributes you want in a mate, a partner. If you are using the Come to Me oil, after your Apple has been dried, apply a couple drops to your Apple, as you rub it over the Apple, ask your guides to show you who you are meant to be with. (If you do not use the oil, just hold your apple, and ask) Use the knife to peel the apple but be extra careful to NOT cut it short or cut yourself. Peel the entire apple. Saying this aloud or to yourself as you go:

"As I peel, please reveal,

The one my soul is meant to see, so we can be."

After you have finished the peeling, take it and throw it over your left shoulder.

The initials of your love will be revealed. If you are lucky enough, you may even see a full name.

## BE GONE POWDER

No one likes an enemy or an unwanted person in their life, it can make it chaotic. A way that people have dealt with this is a quick and easy powder. Some may call it hot foot powder, and some may have their own names like mine which is "be gone" or "go on and get" powder. All have the same result; the unwanted party is no longer around.

I have seen some powders contain toxic items that will cause harm to the party if they put their bare skin against the workings and this one is not that. It doesn't have to be toxic to get the job done but it is completely up to the conjurer how they choose to practice.

### ITEMS NEEDED

- Pepper
- Salt
- Snake skin (if accessible)
- Black salt (optional)

## DIRECTIONS

This is an easy way to keep harmful people away from you and yours. First you start with mixing your ingredients together, it isn't a lot of items but as you stir them together think of your end result, the harmful people cast out of your life.

After it is all mixed together take a moment to take some deep breaths, as you do envision the person you want to leave or the potential drama you want out of your life.

Once you feel it has been charged enough, sprinkle this mixture around your personal areas, such as were you work, your house on the outside to keep unwanted people and energies out, or if you have a target for your "be gone" powder, sprinkle it in their shoes. If you can't get to their shoes, sprinkle it across their path they walk or in their footsteps.

If you have a specific person you want to keep away you can also add that to this mixture, too. Grab dirt from their footprints or their threshold of their door, somewhere they walk daily and add that to your mixture to target a specific person.

The above ingredients are simple, but they can be added to as you feel. The "hot" portion is normally several types of pepper. Just be careful not to harm a person's skin or let them breath it in depending on how hot you would like this powder. Because of this I prefer to stick with the basics, black pepper works simply fine and packs a punch that will get them out of your life and on their own way.

# A CHARM FOR A FEMALE ENERGY

From the beginning of time, women have always thought to be the weaker sex. "Thought" is the key word in that because most of the women I know are stronger having put blood, sweat and tears into raising families, have careers, and being the mother, father, Dr and Lawyer for those they love. I remember seeing a saying when I was young "behind every strong man is an even stronger women" and that has always stuck with me because it is an absolutely true statement, especially with our upbringing.

In olden times, your mother, grandma, maw-maw, or a female that was your elder normally was the center of your world, she was the glue that kept everything together.

Sadly though, she wasn't respected as a male would be, history has shown us that, so this charm is to give the female energies a leg up in negotiations. If you are looking for a promotion, for a rich suitor, or anything to deal with money, this definitely will help, it sways people to your way of thinking.

Works best on masculine energies.

## ITEMS NEEDED

- Come to me oil
- Jezebel Root
- Honey

## INSTRUCTIONS

This is a simple spell to perform but two options to work it.

The first being, an oil you anoint yourself with and the second option is you anoint the root and carry it with you.

The first option is for you to combine the root with your come to me oil, you may even add in a touch of honey or sugar, to sweeten your targets' disposition. Of course, you combine it in a small glass or jar, when you do hold it in both hands and see a white light from above filling the small container with what you want, your end result.

The second option is you put the come to me oil on the Jezebel root and carry it on your left side. You infuse it with the directions the same as with the oil. You program the root to see your end result you are asking for.

Whether you wear it as an anointing oil like perfume or you have the physical root in your pocket, before you leave the house after have gathered yourself and ready to concur the day, take a drop of honey and put it on your lips like gloss, this will sweeten your words on deals you want.

# APPALACHIAN WAY OF TELLING WHAT THE SEX OF AN UNBORN BABY WILL BE

This is a terrific way to predict your unborn baby and I had this done to me when I was pregnant, many moons ago.

When I was pregnant with my son, I went to my aunt and uncle's house for a family gathering. The same aunt that my father watched as the warts disappeared on when they were young was there. She asked if I would like to know the sex of my baby because at that time I had not been told and when she performed this easy gesture, she was able to tell me to expect a boy.

## ITEMS NEEDED

- Needle and thread
- A pregnant woman

## DIRECTIONS

This simple little gesture is quick and easy but very telling. You set the pregnant lady comfortably where she would like with her arms in front of her. Next you take the threaded needle and dangle it above her forearm by the thread, so the needle is able to swing freely. If it swings back and forth it will be a boy, if it circles it will be a girl.

# COME TO ME OIL

Who would not want a little extra push in the attraction department?

This oil is used to bring to you what you are trying to attract, helping it find its way to you. Come to me oil is used as a ritual oil that can anoint candles, give a boost to spells, or can be worn. Before placing it on skin to be worn, make sure that you are not sensitive to any items that are used in this oil.

**Items needed.**

- A carrier oil, personal choice, grape seed
- Clove
- Pachouli
- Load stone- make sure it is fed
- Cinnamon chips or sticks that are broken
- Jar or bottle that is cleansed

**Directions**

Fill jar or bottle ¾ of the way full of your carrier oil. As you place the oil and items into the container, make sure to hold each item and tell it what is needed of it in the works. You are asking to amplify your needs, such as bringing things to you. So, let the items know this request. After meditating and telling the items what is needed of them, place one by one in the carrier oil. Amounts vary with size of container, use your intuition on amounts. Shake container daily with intent to charge.

# CORD CUTTING SPELL

Sometimes we take on extra energy that is not meant as our own. This is a result of toxic people, situations, and occurrences that happen in our lives. If you are more sensitive to energies, a person can also feel weighed down by the world and this spell can remedy that.

**Items needed for the spell:**

- Two white candles
- Twine or cord of your choice that is flammable
- A fireproof container,
- (Preferably a flat surface the candles can sit in)
- Salt of your choice
- Matches or a lighter
- Knife or carving tool

**Directions**

While performing this spell make sure that you follow all safety regulations pertaining to fire. Start with your container to hold your candles, place it on your cleansed area to get started. Pick one of the two candles to represent you in the spell. Once you have done this carve your initials or your full name on the white candle. On the second candle, if you have a target, you can put their name just as you did yours on the first candle.

You can also leave this candle blank for calling all the energies that are meant to be severed from you. After you have attached the two candles to the fireproof container, make sure you leave space that the candles are not touching, roughly about 3-4 inches apart. The easiest way to do this is to melt the end of the candles until they stick to the container. Your next step is to take your twin or cord and wrap from you to the other person or situation. The cord from one candle to the other is signifying the energy exchange that is happening. Go around the outside of the candle workings with salt for a ring of protection. Now is time to light the two candles and watch as they start to burn. As you are watching this, concentrate on pulling your energy back from the universe.

Repeat three times this phrase.

"I call back the energy that is meant to be mine,

I sever all ties with situations, people, animals, and locations that do not serve me."

After you have done this three times, watch the candles until they are completely gone. As you do this meditate on bringing your energies back to you. Once the spell is done, you will feel lighter and free of the weight of the unneeded energy.

Repeat as often as needed.

## HOW TO GET RID OF UNWANTED VISITORS WITH ILL INTENT ON YOUR PROPERTY

In the hectic hustle and bustle of the age now, the one thing I enjoy is being off to myself, unbothered and left to my own devices. Sometimes we need that to feed our souls.

The mountains have always been a place to hide or get away from others, so if someone came into your holler unannounced or unwelcome, they normally would soon be greeted by the stronger, more respected ones in the family and asked kindly to leave in so many words. As a young person I saw this, especially at deer hunting season if someone wanted to "explore" where the deer might be. Now a days, that type of clan protection we don't have as much as in days that have long passed, so we must protect our little piece of solidarity on our own. This is what this working can do, give you peace of mind. This is an old working that has recently been found more in the US as these jars have been unearthed. It originally came over with our ancestors as they migrated into these mountains and lands.

Just as you will notice certain markings on barns and houses to keep evil spirits at bay, it was also used to keep witches away.

This has been adapted into the witch's arsenal of tools also, because every true witch knows that a healer and witch are two sides to the very same coin.

## ITEMS NEEDED

- A jar
- Pins, needles, razor blade, or shattered glass
- Your own water (pee, urine)
- Vinegar
- Candle(optional)

## DIRECTIONS

You are essentially marking your territory and protecting it. No wants people of ill-will on their property or in their space. So, we begin with the jar. Place the jar with the spikes of the pins, nails, glass pieces of whatever you have pointing up towards the lid, as if someone was to open it, they would get the sharp end of the items you placed in it. Of course, if some are not pointed exactly in the same direction, it is all right, just know your intent is what counts. Next you want to fill about one-third of it with vinegar, the acid of it will add to the displeasure of anyone trying to come on your property or anything you own or claim as yours.

Next step will need to be done first of the morning, you are to catch your first morning water (pee or urine). This has your strongest intent in it. Make sure to be thinking of what you want this jar to do, such as keeping people or ill intent away.

Then add it to your jar. You can also spit in the jar for an extra bump of intent also. Now you close the jar to never be opened again. This working you will not open, some may bind the top with candle wax, which you are more than welcome to do but closing it tightly is fine also. Now you want to bury this somewhere on your property. You can do that the furthest or closest to your house as you need. Me personally, if I have a long driveway, I would bury it at the beginning, so no one would start up my driveway with bad intent. Some choose to keep it at their front door, this is completely up to you, and your choice.

Those that live in an apartment or a place where they can't bury something, get yourself a pot that you would have for a potted plant big enough to hold the jar you have made, cover it with potting soil. It is up to you what you put otherwise in the pot such as a fake plant or real. This method is an effortless way to hide your workings in plain sight with no one knowing.

# HONEY JAR

Whether it is a person or a situation you would like to "sweeten" the disposition of, this spell is a quick gentle go to.

### Items needed

- White candle or oil lantern
- Jar or bottle that has been cleansed with lid
- Honey
- Brown lunch bag
- Pen

### Directions

Light your white candle or oil lantern, set your intentions for your workings. Once you are ready, grab your brown lunch bag. Tear it until you have a palm size square. On the brown paper, write with your pen what you would like to sweeten, it can be a person or a situation. Think of the person or your situation while you write this on the piece of paper. Once you are done, fold the paper towards you and clockwise until it is the size that can easily be placed in the jar. Now, it is time for the honey, fill the jar 3/4ths of the way up. Closing the top on the container. If you are using a candle, seal the top of the spell jar with wax, the whole time still seeing your end result. For an extra kick to the spell heat up the jar so the honey is warmed but, slowly so it doesn't harm the container or spell. This is optional but it does make this subtle spell more potent.

## HOW TO BLESS SALT, WATER AND OIL

You will see a lot of these items used in many practices or workings and some will ask to have blessed ones, such as in healings or cleansing. I personally use all three in my cleansings.

The oils I use to have extra protection, just as I do with the salt and the water is a vessel, I use to contain the energies I pull off of people. So, it is always nice to have them blessed to have extra power if you are a person who conjures as such. In a cleansing, I do not know what type of energies I might come across so having a more powerful option is good to have on hand.

How a normal person who doesn't do such things would use these is with salt, if you are using it to banish, you want to have a powerful little punch, oils are good for anointing yourself or your tools when you do rituals and water is an all-around good item to have in spirit work, communication and just an all-around element.

## ITEMS TO US

- Salt with the purpose to bless
- Water with the purpose to bless
- Olive Oil with the purpose to bless

## DIRECTIONS

Make sure that you take each item and have a separate bowl, jar or container that separates it from normal usage, portioned out just to use to be blessed. Whichever you are blessing, you will do this for 3 days, three times a day. The last time a day that you will bless the item will be at 3:33pm which is said to be the time that Jesus saved us from all of our Sins. Some who are reading this will have different beliefs than that of Jesus and that is completely up to the conjurer, so I will address both options on the blessing.

When you are asking for the blessing of the items, this is roughly what you will say, three times, three times a day, for three days.

"Bless this item to be purified in your name, the Father, the Son and the Holy Ghost."

After the third day and third time, it is complete. Make sure in this working that it is only done during the day, with the sun out.

If you are not of the faith that pertains to Jesus, then it can also be blessed with three times a day, for 3 days and these words spoken as you hold the items in your hands to charge with your energy, three times.

"Cleansed and blessed will this item be,

I command by my _____ and me."

*Fill in the blank with whatever your connection with the other side you have such as ancestors, deities, or guides, it is completely up to you *

# HOW TO MAKE A PETITION

A petition is your contraction with the spirit world. A good way to think about it is just a note to make sure everything is understood that is needed. It is a simple way to ask your ancestors, spirit guides or what you choose to work with on the other side of the veil for help and guidance to carry out the spell or working.

## ITEMS NEEDED

- Brown paper bag
- Writing utensil
- Come to me oil(optional)

## DIRECTIONS

I am going to keep the petition simple because there are various things that can be adjusted to make your petition or name paper more intense, such as if you are doing a petition for love, you would use red ink, or if you wanted to encircle a couple you would write in a circle with their names in the middle never lifting your pen and writing your intent around them.

There are so many variables, so we will start at the beginning and simply. Let us start with the paper, you can use whatever paper you like because it is your practice, but what is considered the most authentic is brown, which you can get from what we would call a brown paper bag or a poke. The kind you would pack lunches in back in the day. Tear the bag until you have a small square big enough to write what you need on it. The key to tearing and folding is if you want something to come to you, always turn the paper towards you, (clockwise)if you want something to be away from you, you turn the paper away from you(counter-clockwise).

After you have the size and shape you want, now it is time to write. If you are doing work on someone, or to affect someone, that is your target. You can put as much information as you like on there, but normally you at least want their name, date of birth and location.

John Doe-01/02/33-Kentucky

John Doe-01/02/33-Kentucky

John Doe-01/02/33-Kentucky

As the example shows, write it at least three times, but it can be as many as you want, but make sure at least three. This is why it is also called a name paper. I would like to make sure that I have all the info as above, but I have seen some with just the name on it.

Now to lock down or secure your petition, you can use the come to me oil. You put one drop on your finger and touch it to each corner and in the middle if you have the oil handy if not it can be completed without it. Now if you have any personal items of the target's, you can also add them as you start folding the piece of paper up. Remember, if you are trying to bring something towards you, you fold it towards you and turn clockwise, if you want those workings away from you, you fold away and turn counterclockwise. After the petition is the size you need it to be folded, then you are done. This is a simple petition, it gives the spell, working or conjuring a target, something to aim at.

## HOW TO MAKE A PERSON YOURS UNTIL THEIR ENDS

This spell is not for the faint of hearts and uses blood.

* Blood sharing can be dangerous because of infections and diseases and should be used with caution, if you choose to participate in this, you take full responsibility for your actions*

I have had women confess this being used in hushed words. This is an old remedy to keep a partner yours. Do understand that some of these same women who have told me this have also followed up with saying it has been a rough go of things but at the time they wanted their partners to be theirs and theirs only. A lot of times you will find the woman or man who chooses to use this will be completely in love with the person and they want them to feel the same or the partner they have may have a wandering eye, so they want to keep them all for themselves.

You will find that magick is a beautiful tool but if you force something that was never meant to be yours, it can sour very quickly. Keep this in mind if you decide to use this conjuring. It is simple and powerful. It is also old mountain workings that women mostly have kept to themselves other than sharing in hushed groups.

### ITEMS NEEDED

- Baked items, such as bread or pie work best.
- Blood, for a woman it is most potent from menstrual blood, but any blood will do in a pinch.

### DIRECTIONS

Make your baked good as you normally would, in your mixture add a drop or two to your ingredients before you place in the oven.

Bake and serve as normal.

This will link your partner to you as they consume the baked item.

# HOW TO REMOVE A CURSE

Bad luck is one of the worst things to have in the mountains, it can affect everything from your crops to cattle to just everyday inconveniences. This could be an important thing when your day depends on being able to provide and move through the mountains with ease. The way a person can tell if they have a curse or workings on them is oppression. Now a days there are ways to quickly tell if you are cursed (I have included that in my section) but back in the day, they could also feel this oppression or they could see nothing was going right for them. It's almost as if you feel the weight of the world. Casting, workings, or the evil eye can make a person feel like nothing is going right with them. My sister and I have felt this before. It was as if someone came right up to us and told us we had these workings on us because of how strongly we felt. People would ask us how we knew and if you are a person who can feel these energy flows, you just know. Feelings that are not your own can be impressed onto you also, such as depression and anxiety.

My trusted and true feelings of a curse removal is, what can it hurt, the worst it does is remove your curse, so I would perform them. A

removal also paired with a cord cutting, you can't go wrong with if you feel you need an extra kick to make sure that all the energy or bad intention is cut off. So, if you feel this oppression, feel free to perform this at will and as many times as needed. Some curses and intents are emotionally fueled so they do leave a stronger impression. If this is the case, you may need to redo your curse removal once a month until you feel it is completely gone.

This spell contains lemons. They are something that people could grow and also, they are a cheaper fruit, so they were used in workings a lot. Especially with things that needed to be soured or drawn away. A general piece of advice and disclaimer, if depression and anxiety is present no amount of spell work can replace seeing a professional for these issues. I would recommend anyone eliminate that possibility, no matter how we don't trust doctors in the mountains, there is no substitution for a physician especially when dealing with our mental health.

## ITEMS NEEDED

- One lemon
- Salt (optional blessed Salt)
- Knife

## DIRECTIONS

Find yourself a lemon that you feel would be good for this working. Ideally, you want one that is in good shape so you can transfer what is on you to it. That is what is happening in this removal. You are drawing it off of you onto the lemon.

This can be performed anytime of the month but if you want extra intent do it on the Waning Moon, after the Full Moon, as the darkness pulls the light off the moon so shall this spell remove your curse, when you are at the darkest of the moon, that is time to do workings against your attackers so this will be when the curse remover has ran its course. Do not keep it near you or in your house after the darkest of the moon or the darkest of the moon as our granddaddy would say.

*If you are in dire need of this spell removal, the moon phases do not matter, you can perform it at any time of the month*

Take the lemon, and cut it in two with your knife, take the lemon in both hands with the just cut side facing out towards you. Run the lemon from your head to your toes, making sure to start above your head and definitely get the soles of your feet, especially if you think they have used hot foot powered or "be gone" powder.

You can touch the lemon to your body or use it about an inch or two away from your physical skin. When I do my workings, I touch the skin, but some prefer to do the hands-off approach and it is completely up to the caster. Make sure the clothes you wear is some you don't mind ruining because lemon does have acid in it.

As you are performing this ritual, make sure you are focusing all your intent on getting that curse removed, your breathing should be to "push out" anything that doesn't belong to you. Which means breathing through your diaphragm, your stomach or as some would say "gut." This will get the energy moving around you.

You can say a few words also while you are doing this if it helps you focus such as the following:

"Curse be done,

You aren't allowed to stay long,

Go back to where you came,

With them it should be the shame."

After you feel satisfied with your results, place the two halves of the lemon on a plate or paper plate, take your salt, or blessed salt if you have it and completely cover the top of the lemons that are cut.

Place this in a darker place and let the salt and moon phases work this. Do not think of it again until you remove it at the Dark of the moon to get it as far away from yourself and your loved ones. Burying it at a crossroads NOT near your house would be the best solution but if you just need to rid yourself of it, all the four elements are the best, Fire, Water, Wind and Earth, to dispose of it.

Make sure this is done at night also, we do not want any light getting to this working, that is the intentions or drawing it off.

Now if you did not use the moon phases to help you, this is how you can tell when to get it out of your house, check weekly on the working, if it has started to shrivel and draw up, then the spell is working, but do not go past 2 weeks of it in your house, you have to remember this, the longest is two weeks because of need you to think of it as a sponge, it is soaking in all that curse and bad intent. If that is left in your home or near your loved ones it is what you would consider a curse "bomb". You will notice people will start getting snippy and fighting more. The whole attitude of the house will change. So, you must not let it stay longer than two weeks,

If you see the lemon completely shrivel before the two weeks and you are satisfied and feel the curse lift, it can be disposed of as soon as you would like.

Repeat monthly or as you feel needed.

# HOW TO TELL IF YOU HAVE A HEX, EVIL EYE, WORKINGS OR CURSE ON YOU

If you believe that you have some workings on you, this is a simple effortless way to find out.

## ITEMS NEEDED

- A bowl of water
- Two match sticks

## INSTRUCTIONS

Take the two match sticks, these can be long or short, depending on the size of your bowl. The key is to make sure they fit with ampule enough room to move around in the bowl freely.

Rub the match sticks all over you, from head to toe, making sure not to strike them on anything or your clothes. You will not at any time during this spell light the matches or strike them. (Make sure to follow all safety guidelines pertaining to handling matches)

Once you have done this completely, throw the match sticks into the bowl of water.

Now you have two options at this point, you can give it 5 minutes and read the matches, or you place the bowl under your bed while you sleep over night, when you wake, you pull the bowl out and read it then. Either way is up to the worker.

How to read the match sticks:

-If the sticks are crossed you have workings on you. (The deeper they are crossed the more the curse, hex, or workings have rooted)

- If the tips are touching or they are slightly crossed, this means someone has tried and wasn't as successful as they would have liked, or they are just starting their casting.

-If the two match sticks are separate, you do not have workings on you.

# HOW TO KNOW WHEN A SPELL HAS FAILED OR BACKFIRED

We all do our best to make sure our workings do what they are told, good or bad we want the spell to have the outcome it is programmed for or meant to do. There are some signs that it is not working correctly.

### TIME-FRAMES OF WORKINGS

- Before
- During
- After

### THINGS TO BE ON THE LOOK OUT FOR

#### Before:

How to tell beforehand if your spell work is not going to be good is a couple of ways, first being your mood, if you have been in a horrible mood, such as not able to mentally focus, or just feeling down that will also affect your spell work.

I once did a working for a love potion when I first started out but was going through the worst heart ache I had ever been through.

When I charged the potion, the conjure called for the energy to be filter through my own heart, needless to say we called it "the curse" because it was the saddest love potion you could imagine, it gave all who used it the heartache I had within me. This is a perfect example of knowing if you are in the right frame of mind to perform spell work. Also, if you have signs such as bad omens or broken glass, do not perform the spell then. If you pull cards to see the outcome of your spell, if anything is pointing towards not doing the spell, heed the warning. It is a lot simpler to just replan the spell for a different time than reversing it.

**During:**

If any of your items you are trying to use are broken, spoiled, or rotten. Maybe you have one broken candle in your spell, which is something you should keep in the back of your mind IF you feel the other energy is correct for the spell but if more than one is a miss then you need to really search to see if:

- you know all the facts about the matter
- If all your information that is driving you to perform the spell is correct and accurate
- If this is the right course of action

Emotions are what fuels workings but if you have incorrect information or someone is using you as a pawn in a bigger plan of action these emotions could be focused on the wrong direction. The ones you work with on the other side could be pushing for you to seek answers to questions you may not know you need before proceeding. I was doing a working for a lovely lady who wanted her love to return. What some may not know is magick is a beautiful tool for love if used correctly, it helps what is an ember to be flamed into a fire. So, for a return spell to work, you must have an ember so we can flame it. If it is not there, the target can refuse, and it may make them get angry and pull away even further. The reason being is they feel that pull to come towards the spell work and if this is something they are against then they will fight even harder to get away. This was the case for the conjure I was involved with, I was told there was still a spark on both ends, so I preceded, let's just say she contacted me very quickly when the spell took hold to reverse it. Also take notice of the weather and things around you as your preparing your workings. If you are conjuring and the weather changes drastically, the wind or animals start acting off, take heed to this also. Even if it just doesn't sit with your soul right, this is your working, you are in control of if you proceed. If the spell is meant to be cast, it will happen in time.

### After:

This is a big one because you are going to know, trust me. Your working will not have the outcome you want.

Some signs to look for when your spell has failed or backfired:

- the opposite happens
- you notice more hostility around your house or the place where the spell is located.
- the energy just feels off
- the spell doesn't affect your target but another person
- you start having a string of bad luck

- your target acts the complete opposite or has resentment for the practitioner without knowing of the workings
- there is a heaviness or depressive energy around where the spell was cast.

If you feel this energy or have these things happen, immediately try to stop the workings.

In the case of the lovely lady who wanted to be reconciled with her ex, she contacted me, and everything had gone bad. The opposite of what she wanted had happened, she had a string of bad luck, and even health problems. I advised her on steps to take to destroy the workings and how to get rid of them. I, myself was wondering if everything was performed correctly to my ability and delivered to her with direct instructions that she followed to the letter, where did it go wrong?

I used my gift of sight to see a peak into the target. I saw that he had a love in his heart, I even got the first initial of a name for the lady. I then advised the lovely lady also on being truthful if there was still a spark on both sides, not just hers.

Spell casting can be dangerous for people who aren't truthful or knowledgeable, so always educate yourself thoroughly before you start. Another reason why hers backfired so strongly was because it was a jar spell, that I advised her to bury on her property where it got "fed" meaning a lot of foot traffic, so every time her ex came around it would just drive him further away because it was pulling him in a direction he didn't want to go. This is what happens when spell work has the reverse effect, it can sit and become a spiritual ticking time bomb because it was also being fed his anger and resentment in this case. That energy just sat on the property and attracted other things that weren't meant to be there on the darker side of things. Now of course, not all conjures are going to have this dramatic outcome, it could just not work. Nothing happens, no spiritual bombs, just emptiness. This is an easy spell to deal with. You just dissemble the workings and release the energy attached to it. Your best friend when dissembling a spell is the four elements. They can cleanse and purify the workings.

Always make sure to be conscious of health advisories and guidelines when using the four elements and wildlife.

# KNOT MAGICK

Knot magick is as old as the hills. The one thing you can do to contain things, items or magick is to tie it in a knot. If you want to keep something in place you tie it down and that is just what it is used for. Some say if you need the magick you put in each knot you untie it, and it is released to be at your disposal. Where other beliefs are you use it constantly because it is contained in the knot, either way is completely up to the practitioner.

## ITEMS NEEDED

- String, cord, or twine of the conjurer's choice
- Items to be placed in the knots(optional)

## DIRECTIONS

Start with the twine, cord, or string in your hands, concentrate on what you want from these workings. For example, if it is protection, which is what you concentrate on, and as you get into tying your knots, each time you visualize what protection looks like to you. You can even use color in your string, twine or cord that would correspond such as Black would be used for protection or banishing. After you have decided what your goal is with this charm, you can start your knots, some may want to add certain things to each knot such as a bell, a feather or anything they would feel that adds even more power to the workings, but this is optional of the conjurer. Make sure to do multiples of threes because odd numbers seem to manifest the best but also three is a magical number whether it is Mother/Maiden/Crone, Father/Son/Holy Ghost, Past /Present/Future, or Spirit/You/Ancestors.

Whatever you believe it holds power, so that is why we use multiples of three.

As you tie say these words:

"As I knot so it shall be, contain this magick for me."

Once you have finished your knots, they can be placed at your entrance to your home, on your person or placed somewhere that the magick is needed.

# MIRROR REPELL SPELL

A spell to push back any negative energy or evil eye that is ushered your way. This is a handy way to keep yourself warded at all times. You never know when you will need a little extra protection and this little spell is just the trick to ward off any unwanted energy or bad intent sent your way. The items needed are ridiculously small in comparison to the punch they give in the spiritual world.

## ITEMS NEEDS

- A small mirror that is attached to a piece of jewelry or can be attached to a piece of jewelry to be worn
- Come to me oil

## DIRECTIONS

Place mirror with the reflective surface upwards so you can see yourself. As you gaze into the small mirror take a drop of the come to me oil and place it on your fingertip. As you clear your mind and concentrate on what you would like from this mirror, visualize a beam of protection and cloaking abilities to come out of this little mirror. As you visualize this take the finger with the Come to Me oil on it and draw a protection symbol on the mirror, whether that is a cross, a pentacle or any sigil that you prefer that symbolizes protection, cloaking or reflecting energy. When you draw this on your small mirror, think to yourself or say it aloud.

"As this mirror reflects, it protects, defecting any ill intent for negativity my way.

The one that cast will be the receiver of the intent, for them it was meant."

Say this as many times as you feel needs to be, each time putting more intent in the words, you must say them at least three times.

When this is done wear the little mirror or reflective surface with confidence you are always protected.

# MONEY, MONEY, MONEY OIL

For a simple and easy money spell, this does the trick, and it isn't a hard spell to work because you may already have some of the workings in your arsenal.

## ITEMS NEEDED

- Come to Me oil (workings can be found in my section)
- Little slivers of chopped up money
- Crystal chips for prosperity and wealth (citrine, fools' gold, garnet, ex)
- Glitter, gold and green, optional
- Small glass jar or bottle

## INSTRUCTIONS

This is an easy quick way to access your ability to gain money and prosperity. Your Come to Me oil is an attraction oil. I like to make a larger batch and divide it out for other purposes. You already have your base oil prepared, so I take a smaller bottle or jar and I fill it with my items and then I top it off with my pre-made oil.

The only instructions I have are make sure you take each item before placing it in the jar and tell it what is needed, breath on the items with your intent. After each item is placed in the small jar or bottle you top it with the oil and then hold it in both hands. When you are holding it, ask for this oil to bring prosperity to your life or whatever is anointed with it. The glitter, if chosen to be placed in the bottle also is for the fae or little folk like creatures. Some believe there are magick "runners" these are fae like creatures that run your magick to where it needs to go. As we all know, the little people or whatever you refer to as fairy folk, they love things that sparkle or shine, so this adds extra to the "gold" or "money" look. A lot of our ancestors were of Irish decent in these mountains, so adding a little glitter if we have it now a days never hurt. You can use this oil on yourself for anointing your shoes to point you where the money flow is, so on your items that bring you money such as dice, and cards.

# WHAT IS OK TO USE IN A WORKING, CHARM OR SPELL

You must remember when people that don't have a lot to work with are trying to ward off evil, trying to protect, or make their life better, sometimes the most powerful things are all you have in yourself.

Listed below are things you have that can be used in a spell to enhance it with your intent or your targets.'

## INGREDIENTS

- Your breath
- Your spit
- Your urine (old timers called it your water)
- Your finger
- Your bowel movements
- Your blood

## ITEMS OF YOUR TARGET'S

- Hair
- Nail clippings
- Their signature
- Any personal item of theirs
- A picture

## MEANINGS

This may sound unusual to some, but you have everything you need for both sides of the coin in you, from healing to cursing.

- So, let's take the lighter side of things; to heal, ask for advice or talk to the spirit world, your breath is a key component. Anyone that is a client of mine has seen me breathe into my cards, my ingredients, items, or whisper to them.
- Your spit can transfer the very thing you would say from the good to the bad, so when you add that to your workings, it is very powerful. To some Appalachians spit can cause feuds that can last generations, so be careful to not spit at anyone or on anyone's name unless this intent is true.
- I have seen urine used in workings to cause harm and in workings for protection, it has your intentions in it.
- Your finger is a built-in wand, so be careful where you point it. It can give you a focal point to aim your intent. That is one of the reasons behind pointing out being rude.
- Now the next item on the list is your bowel movements, it sounds rough, and it is. What better way to show your true feelings for someone if you are working a curse or "be gone"

working than to add your waste, something your body is done with and needs no more.

- All the aspects listed above are powerful, they bind you to the spell or workings, but none is as powerful as your own blood. Be careful to follow safety guidelines when pertaining to blood because disease can be transferred, so always be safe. Other than safety guidelines, blood on the spiritual side of things is very potent. One gift that we have that is more precious than others is our blood, it is our life force, so if you choose to use it, be incredibly careful in where you choose to place your power. To put this in perspective, to this day churches celebrate the blood of Christ. Blood is ever lasting.
- And lastly, your Targets' items are used to enhance the spell to give a stronger link to their essence so that the spirit world has a stronger grasp of what is needed, in return will make your spells stronger and more likely to succeed.

# HOW TO MAKE A MAN'S PRIVATES NOTWORK (TO STOP SEXUAL DESIRES)

A lot of times in these mountains life was hard, harder than it should have been. Women were marrying young, our great grandmother married at the age of thirteen, setting up house and tending to babies. One of the worst things that could happen was that your husband, and provider of what little income to the household that was brought in, would leave with another partner. It would make life as the wife unbearable for numerous reasons and a lost love would be at the last of her list. Another reason to make your husbands' downstairs work less on the sexual side would be because of the children. Back in the woods and mountains, birth control was not as widespread as you think, or as it is today. That is why it would be common for a family to have ten, eleven or even twelve children and the mother would be tired. Now these are all good reasons to use this spell, and justified but the world has changed. Even in this changing world, needs are still out there. So, if you have a need for this spell, it is up to you how or why you need it.

As I have stated, I practice 'an eye for an eye' motto but be aware this is on the hexing and cursing side of workings.

## ITEMS NEEDED

- Pickle/cucumber/ anything that resembles a male private part
- Rusty nails/nails/pins or glass pieces
- Name paper/petition
- Anything personal of the targets (optional)
- Knife

## DIRECTIONS

Take your name paper or petition, whichever you would like to refer to it as, (if you need to know the full way to make one, refer to it in my sections) and write the name of the target, and DOB. Do this three times at least. This would be considered a hex or a conjuring that was not meant for you but others, so you turn your petition AWAY from you. Turn it until the name and DOB is vertical. At this time if you want to add extra, write what you want three times across the name.

Ex "John Doe's member does not work"

Or

Ex "John Doe has no sexual needs, no desire"

When you are done with this, instead of folding it towards you, make sure to fold it AWAY from you in a shape that will fit in your vessel you are using for his member (pickle, cucumber, etc.).

Take a moment to get your sharp items together and your petition. Gather all of your intent for this spell, I need you to think of how it feels when you are having to provide, and he is "cattin" around or when you find out you have another unwanted baby coming along. The hardship and struggles. This is what you give this spell, hold the petition and sharp objects in your hands and let the energy that would be weighing on you flow out of your hands, give it to these items. Once that is done, take your vessel, cut it straight down the middle and place the petition inside, if you have any person items at this time you can place it within the vessel, such as hair, nail clippings, spit, whatever you have that will connect him to this conjure. If you don't have anything, your petition will be enough.

After everything is placed inside, you take your pins, nails or your sharp objects and push them into the vessel. Piercing it through the vessel, the petition and out the other side. As you do this, say what this does to you when they follow their sexual desires.

Ex "heartbreaking" "betrayal" "deception" "financial burden"

Once this is all done, take the vessel and bury it, most will at a crossroads, or somewhere that it will get "fed" meaning high traveled area. This may also benefit from being worked on in the dark of the moon. Once you bury it, do not think of it again. Give it over to the spiritual side and watch as the vessel decays so will these sexual desires.

# PROSPERITY JAR

Prosperity can come in numerous ways, such as monetary, career promotions, new business ventures but also in your everyday life of abundance. This spell jar will usher that energy in for you.

**Items needed**

- Cleansed jar that can be sealed
- Citrine stone or small chips
- Gold flakes or gold pieces (gold glitter can be substituted if you are in a pinch)
- Rice
- Petition
- Allspice
- Basil
- Nutmeg
- Cinnamon
- Black eyed peas
- Bay leaf
- Pen
- Green candle

**Directions**

To start this spell, light your green candle and sit with your intentions. Visualize yourself already graced with prosperity and what it would feel like. As soon as this is accomplished, start adding your ingredients together. With each one you place in the jar, hold it in your hands before and let the ingredients feel what it would be like for you to have prosperity. After you feel this has thoroughly been embedded into the ingredient, place it in the jar. At this point, write your petition to suit your situation (how to write a petition is in my previous conjurings if you need instructions on how to preform one)

All items should be inside the jar except the bay leaf and pen. At this time write what you would like with the pen on the bay leaf, still holding onto the feeling of what it will be like when you have the prosperity you want. Place the bay leaf inside the jar, as well, after you have finished with it. Place the lid on the jar and take your green candle that has been burning throughout the ritual and seal the top of the jar. Once the wax has dried, place the jar in a place with a large amount of foot traffic in your house or place of business.

Shaking once a day to energize the spell.

# TO WARD AND PROTECT YOUR PROPERTY SPELL

One of the things a person wants is to feel safe and your home or where you dwell is no expectation. When my sister and I come home and we pass our threshold, we have always felt it was a barrier for unwanted things to not cross. Nothing could pass and the ease and comfort that gives someone is unmeasurable, so this is what this spell is for; safety and ease for you. This spell wards against people or things with ill intent and forces on the magical side of this, such as creatures, elementals, haints and some pests that could be causing inconveniences on your property, such as the fae, or little people or folk as people in the mountains say. Did you ever notice that older properties would have an iron wrung fence in front of their property, this is the same aspect. Iron that is used in this spell is a wonderful ward for not only warding against things of this world but also supernatural beings.

Take note, if you work with fairy energy this spell would not be what you would want.

## WHAT IS NEEDED

- Four pieces of Iron in the form of railroad spikes, nails, and anything you can drive into the ground that is Iron
- The layout of your property or dwelling you want to protect
- Your intention to claim your property as your own

## DIRECTIONS

To prepare yourself, take a moment to sit quietly and close your eyes. As you do, take some deep breaths to clear any energy around you and just be in that moment, calm. Now this is the setting the intent part, which is one of the most important parts, with your eyes closed, think of the borders of your property, with extra intent where the four corners of your property are. See them in your mind's eye as if you were walking them, as you do think of pushing back anything that doesn't belong there, either on this plane or other worldly. After, in your mind's eye, you have visually drawn your lines and cleared your path, say aloud or either in your head:

"Let none pass this line that I have created, none that will do me or those that dwell on this property harm."

In your mind's eye again, with your eyes closed, say this incantation as you walk those same lines you have already cleared and created. This locks them to your intent. Once you feel this is strongly achieved, open your eyes and now the physical part starts.

Grab your four pieces of iron, something to drive them into the ground with and walk to the four corners of your property. At the corners, you will drive these stakes or pieces of iron into the ground and as you do, say the incantation again as you do it. Also, if adding more to the incantation is something you feel, also do that. This is your property and your peace of mind; you can make it your own. Some like to list those to be protected or certain aspects they want that special attention to protecting. Once you are satisfied with the iron being placed in the ground and your intentions, move to the next corner of your property, and do the same, repeat this until all four corners are staked.

Now take a minute once the iron is in the ground and visualize in your mind a barrier such as an electric fence that is glowing and connecting all those irons together and you and your loved ones safe in the middle.

You have completed your warding spell.

If you would like to add more power to this working as you are setting your intentions you can ask your ancestors, guides, God, deities, or other energies beyond the veil you work with to assist in this process. This is not required, but if you would like that assistance, feel free to add it in.

*If you live in an apartment or property that does not have land attached, get four pots and soil, make what would look like a potted plant, you can even add a fake or real plant as long as the iron will not adversely affect the living plant. Do the same ritual just place the four pots with soil in them in the four corners of your dwelling and use them as if it were physical property. *

# BLACK PROTECTION SALT

Salt already has powers of protection but if you feel that you need an extra layer of protection, this spell is for you.

### Items needed

- Black Candle (if Black isn't available, you can use white)
- Regular salt or sea salt
- Crushed eggshells (clean, empty shells)
- Incense or ash from spell work of protection
- Pepper
- Crushed black Obsidian (optional for extra kick)

### Directions

Light your black candle and take a moment to visualize what you would like. Every ingredient you place together ask it to do what you expect, in this it would be for strong protection. One by one as the ingredients are added, blend them together.

Sometimes this salt can also be called Witch's Salt. It can be placed around the home, in your car, in doorways, anywhere you want to keep negativity away. If you suffer from nightmares, you can also sprinkle it around your bed to relieve them.

# ROAD OPENER WORKING

Have you ever felt that you are against the world, that everything is uphill? This would be a good time to make sure that your path that is meant for you is open. Sometimes a person can have obstacles that are not meant to be in their way placed on their path. Whether it be choices or other practitioners who place these hurdles in your way. Also, you will notice if your path is blocked you will not receive the blessings that are meant for you, such as people or things in your life. I use road openers on all my clients that I cleanse. I will share with you how I do them so you can get to the path that is meant for you.

**ITEMS TO USE**

- White candle or lantern
- Come to me oil(optional)
- A quite place
- A direct line of communication with your guides or who/what you work with on the other side of the veil.

## DIRECTIONS

This is one of the last things I do for my clients in my cleansing. I do this at the bottom of their feet. If you are unable to access the bottom of your feet, you can also sit comfortably and focus your energy on your whole being. Light your candle or lantern as a guide for your workings, as a beacon in the night.

You can call on your line to the other side of the veil, whether it be God, Spirit guides, Angels, Ancestors, whatever you feel is your spiritual guidance. At this time, you can anoint the bottom of your feet, your wrists, and the back of your neck or those places you can access with the come to me oil. You now ask whatever is your connection to remove all obstacles in your way and keep you protected on your path. This can be your own prayer; I have one I choose to keep between me and my helpers on the other side and you will have your own too. Call them as you would like any to assist you, make it personal. As you do this look at your path in front of you through your mind's eye, if it has things in your path, keep praying until you see a clear road in front of you.

After you are done, thank your guides that have assisted you.

One thing with workings that is always necessary is you have to be thankful for the gifts and guidance you have.

# SAFE TRAVELS CONJURE

When I was young, visitors would come and stay for weeks, it could be family, friends, or those distant relatives no one seemed to remember except your elders in the family. The one thing that was certain was the travel. When my mother was just a little girl, she would be my great granny's traveling companion, with no cell phones or face time, you had to catch a bus and off you went to stay with loved ones. The amount of trust we had in our families, friends, and the process of traveling back then was amazing to the standards of today. This conjure is to keep you safe on your travels, so we can have that trust in today's world too.

## ITEMS NEEDED

- String, twine, yarn, or anything you can braid.
- Small items from home (1 or 2 items)
- Clip board
- Some of your hair or hair from whoever you want to protect in travels (just a couple strands, not a lot is needed)

## INSTRUCTIONS

Braiding and knotting go hand in hand in the world of manifestation or magick. Braiding is a strong working that is overlooked in our culture today. Indigenous people have been using braids in their hair and their workings to show respect and to manifest, other cultures have done the same.

We are not going to make a large working, this is one you want to be able to be placed in your pocket, your shoe or anything you carry such as a purse, or bag. The idea is to keep it close to you on your travels for a safe return. Gather your string or the main braiding conduit you are using. Lay three strands out in front of you, make sure they are long enough to braid and add items too.

Take the strands of hair you have collected and add them to your three strands. You can wrap it around one of the pieces you are going to braid or however you like but you must make sure it is placed in the braid somehow. Tie a knot at the end of strands to hold it all together and use the clipboard to hold it for braiding. Just like when we were young making bracelets, you place the end that is knotted under the clip to hold it. You are getting ready to start your working, so make sure you have your small items ready to braid in. If you are having a challenging time thinking of things, it can be as simple as a button off a coat, a small vial of dirt out of the yard, or any item small enough from your junk drawer (most kitchens in the south have one of these). You want to address who is on the other side you work with respectfully, this should be a normal practice for your workings, so it should come as second nature. Start braiding your strands and when you cross the strands over, think or say what you want, or you are manifesting in the strand. Let yourself feel what a safe and pleasant trip would feel like. When you get to a portion that feels right to place the small item in your braid, attach it in your braid by either wrapping it around it or through it and continue braiding. Once you have reached the bottom, tie a knot like you did in the top.

Hold the item you have created in your hands and say:

"As I come and as I stay,

Let me have safe travels along the way,

Back home I will return,

Safe and sound with happiness not a concern."

Recite this at least three times. Once you have finished place the item either in your pocket (left preferably but either will do the job), your shoe, (left is a receiving side but like I said before, either will work) or bag you are carrying.

Safe travels.

# SOULFUL CLEANSING BATH

This is the easiest and the first step I use every time I feel the world getting too much. As you make these cords or connections with people and situations, sometimes we take on these challenges of the energy of the situation. That can make us feel as if it was our own responsibility to take care of these situations that have nothing to do with us. I would watch as my grandmother would worry, you may have even heard someone say that someone had "nerves" or "nerve problems" or they "fretted" this meant to say they worry, or this is where the term "worry to death" also comes from. We take responsibility for energy and happenings that is not supposed to be our worry. So, this is the first step in cleansing myself of these feelings. Before I came to realize a bath was more than just getting yourself clean on the psychical side, I walked around with a lot of worries myself and other peoples' emotions on my back or situations I could not change. I suggest a soulful cleansing bath at least once a week to keep you feeling like yourself if you find you "fret" more than most.

## ITEMS NEEDED

- A quite place such as a bathroom with warm water such as a tub.
- Favorite smells, oils, herbs for relaxation(optional)
- A white candle or lamp

## DIRECTIONS

Get yourself situated to be in a peaceful mindset, if this means shutting out the entire world, give yourself at least 15 minutes. You owe yourself this so you can be a better mom, dad, partner and just all-around person. As your family sees how this can affect your mood drastically, they will give you the time you need to yourself. Fill the bath or tub with a warmer temperature of water or however you like it, place your herbs, oil or whatever gives you a peaceful feeling as you bathe in your water. Turn the lights down and light your candle or lantern. When I was young, we didn't have running water, so we would carry water that we heated on the stove to a tub that I stood in and washed. The easy conveniences of the modern world are truly to be enjoyed with a comforting bath like this and I am thankful and grateful for all the little conveniences now. As you submerge in the water, tune everything out, and let your mind wonder, just be in the moment, and soak. Take deep breaths, count to ten as you do and bring yourself to a peaceful state. After you have achieved this, picture where you would like to be or what would bring you the most peace. And enjoy your visions of this. Sit as long as you would like in this state. Once you feel your bath is coming to a close, this is when your work begins. I need you to visualize energy coming down from the heavens, coming into your crown or the top of your head. This energy will flow through your body, think of it as a white light. As it does, let all other energies in your body be pushed out of your hands and feet. In your mind they could also be a different color, such as black, browns, greens, or any color different from white. This symbolizes the energies that aren't meant for you. As you envision this, pull the plug on your tub. Set in the water as all of it goes down the drain and see in your mind's eye all the different color energy that came out of your hands and feet go down the drain also. As the last drop does down you should feel the release. Now you can go about as you would finishing your normal bath and feel lighter to face your day.

If you do not prefer baths, you can also do the ritual in the shower.

## TO GET RID OF BAD ENERGY IN YOUR HOUSE

There is a reason that Spring cleaning is something that people do every spring because it is moving all of the stale energy out from the winter months to usher in the good energy.

If you have gloomy energy in your house or just want to usher in the new and out with the old this is a simple but effective way to move all that stale, depressing energy out.

### ITEMS NEEDED

- Broom
- Salt

### DIRECTIONS

Go throughout your house and sprinkle salt on the floors. As you are doing this, open all the windows and doors.

Start from the back of your house at the furthest corner from your front door and start sweeping.

Sweep all that salt and energy, driving it towards the front door, as you go by, shut the windows and doors as you sweep through the rooms until you are left at the front door. Now make sure you sweep all the salt and energy right out until you hit dirt.

The ground and salt will absorb all the bad energy and ill intent.

To keep the bad energy from creeping back in, make sure to sweep at your doors, such as your porches and doorsteps at least once a week and if you feel Salt is needed you can add them at your doorsteps also.

This is good for new houses too, before you bring all your family and energy in, make sure to push all of the old out.

## TO HIDE SOMEONE FROM SPELL WORK

Have you ever wanted to protect someone or something from bad workings or the evil eye? Sometimes you can feel someone's bad intentions, it rolls off them like smoke down a valley. So, if you know that someone is up to no good, the one thing I would want to do is protect my family and loved ones. That is the same reasoning behind having locks on our doors, just in case you need them, they are there. Mirrors in the mountains hold a key and portal to the other side of the veil. There are all sorts of superstitions and lore about them. So just as they can open doorways, they can hide things too. In this spell you will find a way to "hide" your loved ones from harm.

**ITEMS NEEDED**

- Two small mirrors, identical
- Brown name paper
- Pen
- Anointing oil or Olive Oil
- Red string

## INSTRUCTIONS

To get started, prepare your state of mind, if that means lighting some candles, just putting yourself in a meditative state or just some deep breaths, get yourself there. While you are getting your mind and body ready, make connections with your guides, ancestors, or those you work with on the other side. Once this is ready, you start with your petition, write your loved one's name on the petition three times. The more detail the better, you can even throw in their birth date. Turn the name paper towards you and write over top, something like "no harm to thee, because your enemy can't see" or something as simple as "invisibility for you to all bad intention," but it also must be wrote three times over the name. Whatever you choose, you can put in your own words, just make sure it covers the points of this which is to make your loved one invisible or cloaked to bad intention or spell work. After this is done to your satisfaction you can either leave the paper flat if it is small enough or fold it towards you, but it must only be a couple times to make it still feel thin because it is going to go in between the two mirrors. The mirrors must lay flush up against each other, no gaps.

Now you lay both mirrors facing up with the reflective surface facing up. Take your oil and lock the mirrors, which means you ask no harm to come through them. You take your finger and put the oil on the tip and draw a symbol of protection, this can be anything you choose, from a Cross to a Sigil. Ask those you work with on the other side to help you place these safety measures in place. Once this is done take the two mirrors facing outward and place the name paper in between, after you do make sure they are flat together. Take your red string and encircle the mirrors and tie them together, when you do, knot the string, visualizing the working you are preforming and how protected your loved one will be. Do this nine times in total. Once this is done you place the bound mirrors in a secure place.

## TRUTH SPELL

The trouble with the truth is sometimes people don't want to see it. If that is the case, this spell isn't for you. But if you would like to command someone to be honest to you, this spell is just up your alley. Do understand that compelling someone to tell the truth against their will is harder workings and you will have to find if that is something in your wheelhouse of conjuring. This spell has a little twist to it. We all know that one person that can fib with the best of them, and not blink an eye. So, this little working has a way of you telling when they are lying. This spell is to enchant an item that will compel them to tell the truth but if they are determined to still lie then it will let you know when they are lying by what you ask.

## INGREDIENTS

- Candle- any color, white is the best
- Item you have chosen to enchant (it can be a hag stone, a truth telling stone such as Lapis, blue sapphire, or whatever you feel pulled to)
- Dominating oil, Come to Me oil or you can use olive oil
- Thyme
- Clove powder
- Knife
- Brown paper for petition
- Pen
- Lighter

## INSTRUCTIONS

This spell is all about the intention you have to see the truth and calling on your guides, ancestors or who or what you are attached to on the other side. I am going to show you how I would enchant this, but you can adjust parts to fit you, such as the "tell" that you enchant the item with. First, set and feel what it feels like to be lied to. Deception, let down and the dishonesty. Once you have the grasp of the emotions, take your candle and knife or whatever you would like to crave the candle with. You write your target three times on the candle, their full name. The more accurate the stronger the bond. Once that is done, gather the oil you will use.

This is where you need sigh deep to focus that feeling of dishonesty, put 3-4 drops of the oil in your hands and rub them together, warm the oils up, put your intention of wanting the truth to be told in the oil. Once you feel comfortable with your oils you rub them on the candle you have carved. You can ask your guides or who you work with, "let this oil guide the way for the light to shine on the truth from this candle" as you rub the oil into the candle. Next place your thyme and ground cloves on your petition paper and roll the candle on it, you can say to your guides, "with these workings, let the truth be told." Once finished, lay your candle aside for a moment. Now we make our petition. Write your targets name three times on the name paper. The next part is up to you and your casting, you want to write across their name, Ex. "stop the lies" if this is what you choose, then you turn the petition AWAY from you because you want them to stop their lying, so you want their lies away from you, but if you are asking for the truth, such as you write 3 times over them, "tell me the truth" or "bring me the truth", you want to fold the petition TOWARDS you. After you have finished working your petition, fold it, and put it in a fire safe container and burn it. As you do address your guides, ancestors or who you work with, as you do feel that letdown of being lied to, this passion is what fuels this working more. Ask them in your own words something as follows "let me be told the truth by <u>target</u>, as this flame ignites this petition please grant my humble request, but if not and target still lies, then let me be shown by a cough from target, as the lies get stuck in their throat."

Once the ashes from your petition are cooled, rub them on your candle also. Now it is time to light your candle. Once you do sit and gaze into it, see in the flames you being told the truth or a cough to show they are lying. If you have someone who is so accustomed to lies, you may have to take the cough instead of the truth. After you sit with your working and you feel the energy of your spell, bring the item you chose to be the truth barrier for you, your stone. Now you can let it go with the candle and petition but if you want an extra kick grab your stone and place it in both hands, then raise it to your lips to breathe your request into it. Think of all the light from your candle entering your stone and you breathe your request, asking that if this stone is present then your spell will be cast on your target. After the candle has burnt down and you feel the spell has taken hold. Place the stone in your left pocket of your pants or somewhere on your left side, which is your receiving side. You will fuel your stone and the petition as you keep the stone on your body.

# TO MAKE YOUR ENEMY CAUSE THEIR OWN DOWNFALL

*Some may say this is darker workings*

This spell is NOT for someone who has a karmic based system they follow unless they are willing to take on the karma of it.

In the mountains, like I have stated before, some of us practice by an eye for an eye, but it also has an understanding for how far is too far. If someone crosses you, you wouldn't want to retaliate with casting for death. Most live by a balance, hence an eye for an eye. Your spell work is your own path, this is the knowledge of how to perform the spell, it is up to you what you do with it.

This spell is meant to bring about your enemies' own demise at their own hands.

## ITEMS NEEDED

- Name paper
- Iron nails/coffin nails
- Honey/ syrup/ sugar
- Hammer
- Ant hill

## INSTRUCTIONS

*Be careful when working with insects that you may have an allergic reaction to, may sting or bite, use your own discretions, safety precautions and know your limits*

This working can be performed whenever you would like, but if you want it to be veiled, do it at night, the darker the better.

Make your name paper short and sweet, just your targets name three times, if you do not want to have a name paper, use an item of theirs, such as a handkerchief or something small of theirs.

Pour honey, syrup or sugar (which ever you want to use) on the name paper or item of your target and nail it to the ground by an active ant hill. You would want to make sure to use coffin nails but if you don't have any of those, you can substitute with iron nails.

As you hammer it into the ground the intentions of this spell is to trick or sweeten the target into being their own down fall, so you can concentrate on that energy and if you would like you can add spoken words of your situation as you hammer the nail into the ground. As the ants eat the working, the target will fall to their own weakness. To add extra intent on the situation, think of the harm your enemy has done to you, imagine what it will be like for them to fall to their own doings, as you do this, let your mouth fill up with spit. Once you are satisfied with the energy behind your thoughts, spit onto the item nailed to the ground by the ant hill.

Walk away leaving the rest with your enemy.

# HOW TO RETRIEVE SOMETHING THAT IS LOST, A CALL BACK CONJURING

This is for anything you have lost that you want called back to you. When you own things and they are misplaced your energy is still on them, they have bonded to you.

## INGREDIENTS

Your guides or who you work with on the other side.

## DIRECTIONS

If I have miss placed something or something is stolen from me, I sit with that feeling. I call in all my guides or ancestors, whoever I work with. I use my mind's eye to see the item, I feel the item, I picture it in my mind and what it looks like. I focus on every detail, and what it would feel like in my hand. And then in my mind's eye, I see what is around it, when I do this, I try to focus on where that is, is it a location, is it a place in my house? I try to figure out what I am seeing. You may get messages that tell you where it is, such as you may hear, "in the draw" or you may get pictures, however the other side wants to relay the message.

If an item has been stolen from you, feel the energy of it, just as the technique before but this time, try to focus on a location outside of your house. You may be pulled to driving to a location, whatever you feel, you follow. Then as you near your items you make feel the energy start to make you either tingle or almost like a vibration.

Someone stole all my Tarot decks out of my vehicle and threw them on the side of the road, I called them back to me with this technique and I was able to feel them in a field and in a ditch. I was able to recover all of them and I still use them today.

# FULL MOON MANIFESTATION WORKING

This working is for what you need, not just what you want. Every time I have used this spell, I have received what I needed not necessarily what I thought I wanted at the time. Looking back, the other side heard my soul loud and clear. If I had known how things were going to be moved in my life, I may not have asked for things as I did, but because I didn't know how it would move me. Movement can be scary when you are not ready to let go of your current situation, think twice before using this. I was ready to receive what I asked for, I just didn't know the other side had been waiting longer than I knew to love me from my situation. So, it happened fast.

### WHAT IS NEEDED

- Your intent for a different situation
- The full moon

### DIRECTIONS

Normally, time and moon phases can be added into a spell, but I always let those know who need something quicker than waiting for a certain time that workings can be done when needed. This working has always been performed in the full moon, and this spell I believe needs that aspect to work. So, if this is unobtainable, this spell isn't got you. Sit with what you want, really think how you would feel or how your life would be impacted, for example, if you ask to be happy. See your happiness, feel what would make you happy, feel that you already have it. Be aware, tears can come when your heart desires happiness also, if you feel that you are not in that situation now, give this all to the moon. Go somewhere you can bask in the moonlight. I enjoy being outside to feel the full effects, but whatever you can do will work.

Tell the moon all those feelings, release them to it, as you do, plead your case of what you would like to feel or how you want your life changed. Be aware if there is someone standing in your way of this, the other side will move them out of the way. So be prepared for change. Once you have released all those emotions and feel the other side has heard your plea, thank them, whoever you work with for their help and watch the changes come.

## STRESS RELIEVER

Stress can be a very heavy burden to carry, so here is a technique I advise all my clients. No special things are needed, just yourself. Gather yourself somewhere you can have a moment to yourself and take a deep breath. As you breathe, take deep breaths in through your nose and exhale out of your mouth. As you do this think of a white grow or light coming from the heavens, continue concentrating on your breathing. Once you have the white light, start filtering down through the top of your head, flowing through your body. This is all done through your mind's eye. Now concentrate on shifting your breathing to when you inhale you use your diaphragm, which is your stomach. Closing off the white light filtering from the heavens, just concentrating on your breathing still, into your diaphragm and out. As you inhale, push the energy out of your diaphragm. Envision this as the white light coming out as your stomach, pushing forward, as it does let all your stress flow out with the white light. After 5 to 10 minutes of this you will feel like a new person.

# RONDA CAUDILL

## RONDA'S MAGICK

Appalachian Granny Women are unique because they are so eclectic. They practice a blend of magic that was created by their ancestors who brought magic from their home countries such as Ireland, Scotland, and England. They combined this magic with the magic of the Native Americans in the Appalachian Mountains, the magical practices of Germans who migrated to the area and magical practices of Africa brought to the Appalachia's by slaves. This eclectic blend of magic is what makes up Appalachian Mountain Magic. These women were invaluable in their communities; they were dowsers finding wells for their neighbors, practiced divination by reading tea leaves and coffee grounds, they were midwives delivering babies and tending to the needs of women, they also made herbal remedies for the sick.

Due to geographic seclusion and poverty doctors were hard to come by so these Granny Women would treat illnesses for their family, friends, and neighbors with Appalachian Mountain Magic. These old-time remedies were handed down and continue to be handed down to select family members who carry on the tradition. These women are also knowledgeable about herbs, gardening and harvesting, animals, cooking and putting food up for the winter. They plant, garden, harvest and put food up according to the signs (moon phases, certain days, etc.).

Appalachian Mountain Magic often uses natural objects such as roots, herbs, stones, bottles, animal bones etc., to provide physical evidence of their magical power. These objects are used in cauldrons, poppets, amulets, jars, etc. to hold your spell. Granny Women of the Appalachians would use the above mentioned but would also employ the use of mirrors, candles, charms, horseshoes, ropes, bells, and salt. These Granny Women were extremely poor and did not waste anything. They made use of anything and everything they had. They would use corn husks for poppets, salt for protection, old bottles to store a spell in, old pieces of tattered clothing to make poppets from, etc.

My heritage has deep roots in Appalachian Mountain Magic handed down to me from Granny Women in my family. My ancestors came to the Appalachian Mountains from Germany, Ireland, and Scotland. I have Native American ancestors. I was born and raised in these mountains and the magick of them lives within me. My lineage is rich with magical people including Granny Women, water witches, Native Americans, psychics, and an ancestor that was tried as a witch in Andover Massachusetts during the Salem Witch Trials. This eclectic group of ancestors are exactly what makes a Granny Woman because the Appalachian Mountain Magic that they use is eclectic magick.

This magick has been handed down through the generations until it finally was my turn to learn and hand it down. Various family members have handed down all these things to me. Now I am teaching my children and grandchildren. One of my grandmother's and two aunts were table tippers practicing mediumship. One of my great-great aunts was a healer (Granny

Woman), whose specialty was removing warts with cat's whiskers. I also had a great great-great grandmother who was a witch and proudly called herself witch. I had a great-great grandfather who was a water witch and dowsed for wells. One of my grandmother's taught me old time home remedies such as, putting coal soot on swollen lymph glands to reduce the swelling, blowing smoke in the ear of a child with an earache, and putting tobacco and water mixture on a bee sting are just a few examples.

I am very proud of my Granny Woman heritage and my connection to these Appalachian Mountains. They speak to me; they are a part of me. They are magical therefore I am magical.

# RONDA'S SPELLS

1. Spell to protect you Grimoire or book of shadows — 212
2. Spell to Protect a Witch's home — 214
3. Witch Bells — 215
4. Upside down Horse — 216
5. Witch's Broom — 218
6. Tie a Red Ribbon — 219
7. Threshold Protection Spell — 220
8. Triple Circle Protection Chant — 221
9. Alter Blessing — 222
10. To see the unseen — 223
11. Get what you want — 224
12. Spell to make someone see the error of their ways — 225
13. Banish Spell — 227
14. Bottle Trees — 228
15. Bring True Love Spell — 229
16. Binding Lovers Spell — 230
17. Invisibility Poppet Spell — 231
18. Mirror Spells — 232
19. Scrying — 233
20. Reversal Spell — 234
21. Reversal Spell for something specific — 235
22. Money Multiplying Spell — 236
23. Take care of your own Issues Spell — 237
24. Threats and Dangers Mirror Spell — 238
25. Invisibility Mirror Spell — 239
26. Mirror Spell for Beauty — 240
27. A Witch's Binding Spell — 241
28. Appalachian charm to protect against other Witches — 242
29. Colored Candle Protection magick while Sleeping #1 — 243
30. Colored Candle Protection magick while Sleeping #2 — 244
31. Spell to calm a cranky baby — 245
32. To get rid of a wart — 246
33. Cherry Tree love Spell — 247

# SPELL TO PROTECT YOUR GRIMOIRE OR BOOK OF SHADOWS

**Items Needed**

- Your Grimoire or Book of Shadows
- Ink pen or quill and ink
- Rosemary
- Salt

Since your Grimoire or Book of Shadows is a sacred and personal and most import of books you need to keep it from being discovered. No witch wants the contents of that book to ever be shared with just anyone. It is a book to be passed down from generation to generation. So, to keep prying eyes from the book do the following.

Hold your book close to your heart and concentrate on your intent; that being to protect your book from anyone who is not invited to look upon it. Open it to the flyleaf and sprinkle a bit of rosemary and salt on the pages.

Say this spell aloud as you write it in the front of your book.

"Elements protect this book from wondering eye and prying look.

And fill it with thine ancient power in this right and ready hour."

Shake lose rosemary and salt from the pages. It's okay if some bits remain; in fact, that's a good thing. It will give added protection.

# SPELLS TO PROTECT A WITCH'S HOME

**Items Needed**

- Salt
- Brick dust (optional)
- Graveyard dirt (optional)

Salt all doors and windows for 24 hours to seal your houses of unwanted guests, spirits, and evil.

Do this by simply taking salt of your choosing and sprinkle a small line of salt under your door mat at all of your exterior doors and in your window seals. You can mix the salt with graveyard dirt and brick dust if you would like for added protection.

Recite the following spell as your sprinkle your salt:

"Unwanted and evil from my home stay away. Never darken my doorstep any day."

After 24 hours you may sweep the salt away or you can leave it until it blows away. You can also put the salt in a small jar and hide it away in the four corners of your home and recite the same spell for added protection.

# WITCH BELLS

## Items Needed

- Red ribbon
- Small bells

Tie small bells onto one or more pieces of red ribbon and fashion them together in a manner of your choosing. While stringing your bells together consider your intent. Hang witch bells to the doorknob with a red ribbon to keep evil and unwanted guests out. It also clears negative energies of spirits and guests as they enter your home and keep your home clear of negative forces.

Recite this spell:

"Guard our home, bell on the door, let evil spirits come no more. Evil spells shall not be cast. And good fortune shall ever last."

Hang a set of witch bells to all exterior doors for added protection.

# UPSIDE-DOWN HORSESHOE

**Items Needed:**

- Horseshoe

Irish lore about lucky horseshoes were brought to the Appalachian Mountains, where most homes still participate in this practice. The story behind the horseshoe is that once the Devil went to a blacksmith to have his hooves shoed, the blacksmith tricked him and nailed red hot shoes to the Devil's hooves, and they were so painful that the Devil tore them off and ran away. It is said that the Devil will come nowhere near horseshoes now. So, people will protect themselves from the Devil by hanging the upside-down horseshoe above their door. The reason that the horseshoe is considered lucky is because it was made by a blacksmith who had a very prosperous trade and because the shoes were magickal because they were forged from metal and fire. Hang a horseshoe upside-down above your door for; blessings, luck, and protection from evil. There are no words needed to be said for this spell.

# WITCH'S BROOM

**Items Needed**

- Broom (Ritual broom)

The Appalachian practice of placing a broom by your front door to warn of company is still common. This was a practice in New England that found its way here to the Appalachian Mountains several hundred years ago that we have adopted.

Simply place an upside-down broom by the door that is most frequently used. If it falls for seemingly no reason company is coming.

There is no written spell for this; the action and intent of placing the broom in this manner and spot is all you need to do.

# TIE A RED RIBBON

**Items Needed**

- Red Ribbon

Tie a red ribbon to your exterior doorknobs to keep unwanted guests away. This is a longtime practice that is still a common in the Appalachian Mountains. In many traditions red ribbons are attached or tied to something or someone for luck and protection.

All you need is a red ribbon and simply tie them to all exterior doorknobs.

Recite the following:

"Red ribbon keep the unwanted away. Only family and friends may enter and stay."

# THRESHOLD PROTECTION SPELL

**Items Needed:**

- Three cloves
- A handful of sea salt
- A handful of rosemary

Stir everything together in a bowl and leave it on a windowsill during the night of a full moon. Then take the bowl outside and spread the mixture outside of your front door and any other doors of your home. The door you use the most should have the most mixture spread. For added protection sprinkle a little on each windowsill too.

There is no written spell required; only the action and intent are required.

# TRIPLE CIRCLE PROTECTION CHANT

**No Items Needed**

This spell can be used for anytime you want or need protection. This spell is usually cast before working with spirits or conducting spell work with Deities or other supernatural beings.

Visualize a triple circle of purple light while chanting… "I am protected by your might, Oh gracious Goddess Day and night. Three around the circles bound and evil sink into the ground."

# ALTAR BLESSING

**Items Needed**

- Rosemary
- Salt

Every witch needs to protect her (his) altar. This is a simple spell for altar blessings. Sprinkle a bit of rosemary and a bit of salt over your altar. Wave your hands over your altar while chanting…

"From the mystic light to fertile foundations. On the shores of waters. Out of the hopes and dreams. On the wings of the Divine. Of light and inspiration. With the inner flame kindled. Divine spark and back to light. For manifestation swiftly fulfilled. Moves the unseen by the moon, the stars, and the sun. By the gods, the goddess and the ancient ones. Blessed be this altar and all here for the good for all and harming none."

You may then dust your altar or leave the bits of salt and rosemary for a few days for added blessings.

# TO SEE THE UNSEEN

**No Items Needed**

To be able to see spiritual and supernatural beings recite the following to them. Concentrate on the beings you wish to see as you say the spell.

"In this tween hour I call the sacred power.

I stand here alone and command the unseen to be shown.

In innocence I search the skies.

Enchanted are my newfound eyes."

# GET WHAT YOU WANT

## Items Needed

- Horseshoe
- Red Candle
- Lighter
- Paper
- Quill
- Ink

Take a horseshoe and ring it around a red candle. Put the candle and the horseshoe in a darkened room in the middle of a table. Write what you desire on a piece of paper with a quill dipped in black ink chant the following as you write.

"What I want I write here. Please take my dream and bring it near. What I want is what I should get. And all my dreams will now be met."

Take the paper and fold it into a square of four creases. Hold it over a flame with tweezers and let it burn completely. Picture yourself with your wish fulfilled. As you burn the paper, send vibes of love at the image you conjure for yourself.

# SPELL TO MAKE SOMEONE SEE THE ERROR OF THEIR WAYS

**Items Needed:**

You will need Something of the person you are casting for or against…

- blood, hair, nails, etc.
- Rosemary
- Thyme
- Mint
- Lemon

Burn in a cauldron all of these things and recite the following spell three times:

"Sands in the North, rich soil beneath. Three times three let them see, let them see. Winds from the East blow through the trees. Three times three set them free, set them free. Fires in the South awaken from sleep. Three times three. Waters from the West set them free, set them free. The errors of their ways let them see, let them see."

Collect the ashes from the Cauldron and bury the remains where there is heavy foot traffic.

# BANISH SPELL

## Items Needed

- Cayenne
- Eucalyptus
- Feverfew
- Mandrake
- Mug Wort
- Peppermint
- Rosemary
- Wormwood
- Your DNA

Cast a circle (Widdershins). Put all the ingredients in a cauldron and burn them while reciting this spell: "That which brings me down I banish. The negative in my life will now vanish. I no longer need it to hold me back. A heavy energy pushes me back. So mote it be!" (Recite three times).

# BOTTLE TREES

## Items Needed

- Colored bottles
- Tree

Bottle trees are an old form of Appalachian folk magic that originated in Africa and is still frequently used. They're placed near houses to protect homes from evil spirits. Bottles of any color can be used; however blue bottles seem to be a favorite. Place the bottles onto bare tree branches, with the neck facing toward the trunk or they can be tied to the tree limbs by a piece of twin or jute. At night, malevolent spirits are caught in the bottles and are believed to be destroyed in the sunlight the following day and on windy nights the spirits can be heard moaning in agony. Bottle trees are steeped in antiquity and are related to the occult belief of genies being trapped in bottles.

# BRING TRUE LOVE SPELL

**Items Needed**

- Love spell herbs, crystals, oils, etc.
- Bay leaf

Add ingredients in a cauldron and burn them while reciting the following.

"Bring true love fast. Bring a love that will last. By night and by day, hear these words that I say. Make my wish be known, as above so below. Earth, Water, Air and Fire Hear my heart's desire. Bring a lover to my door who will love only me forever more. Bring my happiness today, hear these words I say. By Earth, Water, Air and Fire, grant my heart's desire. With harm to none, so shall it be done."

Can be used with candle, cauldron, jar poppet, etc.

# BINDING LOVERS SPELL

**Items Needed**

- Rope or jute

Tie knots in a rope while saying the following:

"On this day, the words I say to bind you and your love to me from help from below and above. I call upon the moon and the stars that only I will be on your mind and in your heart. To all others you reject. I am your only love object. Heart beating only for me. My face is all that you see. My love all you desire. Earth, Wind, Water and Fire. Only excitement for me makes you grow. No one else you can ever know. No one else gives you rise. To try only causes demise. You are consumed by your love for me. I tie these knots by three. I bind thee to me forever and always. So mote it be!"

Carry, burn, or hide away the love knot rope.

# INVISIBILITY POPPET SPELL

**Items Needed**

- Poppet
- Mustard seeds
- Items to decorate the poppet

Create a poppet to carry in your pocket. Put nine mustard seeds in the poppet. Then stuff, seal and decorate the poppet to represent you. When you carry this poppet, you will be unnoticeable by most spirits and most people as well.

# MIRROR SPELLS

Mirrors used for spell work or scrying should always be covered. Once they are used in this manner, they become portals. Simply covering mirrors that have become portals with some type of cloth prevents spirits from coming through them. Covering mirrors in the house after someone has died have been a long practice in certain cultures to prevent the dead from getting trapped in them. This is a practice in the Appalachian Mountains brought over by the Irish and Germans. You can always use oil on your magical mirrors instead of covering them if you prefer. Take a tiny bit of oil of your choosing (I use a protection oil) and mark a tiny X in a tiny spot unobtrusive spot on the front of the mirror. Another important note about mirrors is they will also become portals if you place two facing each other. So always be careful not to hang mirrors directly across from one another.

# SCRYING

## Items Needed

- Black Mirror

Paint the back side of a mirror black or paint the back side of a piece of glass. This is used to scry with. You will be able to see the future and contact spirits by scrying into the blackened glass. Let your eyes go out of focus and open your mind. You may see images with your physical eyes or your third eye. This takes a lot of practice and patience; it's not easy to master. Call upon your ancestors and guides to help you receive visions.

Appalachian Granny women would sometimes scry with water as well. They would help a young girl see what her husband would look like by leaning them backwards over a well or some other body of water and holding a mirror in front of them. They would see the reflection of their future husband in the water through the mirror. They would also peel an apple and drop the peeling into a bucket of water to reveal the initial of the first name of the girl's future mate.

# REVERSAL SPELL

**Items Needed**

- Mirror

Pick a small mirror from a craft store, thrift store, etc. (I like to find my mirrors at antique or thrift stores.)

Smudge it with protective oil and recite the following spell: "Mirror, Mirror, in the light, send it back and make it right."

Then find a permanent spot to place your mirror in a lighted area (not in direct sunlight, otherwise it will reflect the sun and could cause a fire.) This spell can be used for anything you need to reverse.

# REVERSAL SPELL FOR SOMETHING SPECIFIC

**Items Needed**

- Two mirrors
- Paper and pen

Write on a piece of paper the name of the person who cursed you or did you wrong. Place the paper between two mirrors and tie them together with reflective sides facing each other. This sends the curse or wrong doing back to this person.

# MONEY MULTIPLYING SPELL

**Items Needed**

- Large denomination bill
- Two mirrors
- Prosperity oil, crystals, herbs, etc.

Take a large denomination bill and place it between two mirrors and tie them together with reflective side facing each other. Anoint the mirrors and the bill with a prosperity oil. You can also add prosperity crystals, herbs, etc. to the mirrors. Visit the mirrors often daily and think about the money that will be coming your way. Also replenish herbs and oils as needed to keep them fresh.

# TAKE CARE OF YOUR OWN ISSUES SPELL

### Items Needed

- Poppet
- Paper and Pen
- Two mirrors

This spell is for someone who is constantly looking for others to bail them out and do them favors, borrow money, etc. If you are tired of dealing with a person, cast this spell.

Make a poppet that represents this person. Write their name on a piece of paper and if you have a photo put the name and photo inside the poppet. Place the poppet between two mirrors reflective sides facing each other and tie the mirrors together.

Recite this spell:

"You've tarried too long and waited too late; all the support has turned to hate. Sort yourself out before you return, else your bridges will surely burn."

# THREATS AND DANGERS MIRROR SPELL

**Items Needed**

- Mirror
- Eucalyptus oil

To have a heads up on threats and dangers before they happen to you try this mirror spell. Get a mirror and anoint it with eucalyptus oil. Recite this spell while scrying into the mirror. "Mirror, Mirror, hear my plea, let me see danger before it happens to me."

Do this at least once a day to see daily threats and dangers. I have done this to a bedroom mirror and cast this spell each morning before I start my day.

# INVISIBILITY MIRROR SPELL

**Items Needed**

- Small poppet
- Mirror
- Tape, Velcro, etc.

To be unnoticed by people you want to avoid try this Mirror spell.

Make a small poppet representing yourself and attach it to the back of a mirror; tie it, glue it, Velcro it, etc. Recite this spell: "As I go through my day, I will only be noticed by the ones who have my say. To the ones I do not choose the sight of me they will lose."

Recite this daily while starring into the mirror and thinking of the distinction of those you wish to be noticed by and those who you do not.

# MIRROR SPELL FOR BEAUTY

**Items Needed**

- Mirror of any size

Remember in *Snow White* how the mirror would tell the witch she was the fairest of them all (well until Snow White came into the picture). Well, this spell is like that without the talking mirror.

You will enchant your mirror to reflect only your deepest beauty back to you; to boost your confidence and let people see this beauty as well. Anoint your mirror with rose and lavender oils.

Recite this spell before you begin each day:
"Mirror, Mirror, hear my plea, let me see only the fairest part of me. Let my flaws drop away and let others also see me this way."

# A WITCH'S BINDING SPELL

**Items Needed**

- Nine pieces of red yarn or ribbon

Braid nine pieces of red yarn or ribbon that have been braided together. Then tie nine knots in it as you recite this spell: "I knot this string knotting you three times three. I bewitch you, witch, so you can harm no more."

Tie the knotted braided yarn or ribbon in a tree for nine days. Some like to leave it until it rots completely.

# APPALACHIAN CHARM TO PROTECT AGAINST OTHER WITCHES

**Items Needed**

- Seven black cat hairs

On a Saturday at midnight take seven previously plucked hairs from a black cat and tie them together with three knots. While doing this recite the following spell: "This hair that is knotted so knots you. With the tying of this knot so I bind you."

Carry the hairs in your pocket to protect against other witches. They cannot come near the hair.

# COLORED CANDLE PROTECTION MAGIC WHILE SLEEPING

**Items Needed**

- Green candle
- Black candle
- Salt

Appalachian granny women use various colored candles strategically placed in their homes for protection against anything evil that tries to enter through doors or windows. For instance, many old homes were built way before forced heat with heat vents in each room. So, when they built these houses, they would put a window above every interior doorway so that they could open the windows to circulate cool night air around the house in the summers and wood stove or fireplace heat during the winter without having the bedroom doors open.

**Spell 1:** In bedrooms they would put a green candle in the outside of these windows above the doors of the bedrooms and be lit on them to protect whoever is sleeping in the room from harm caused by evil spirits who try to enter through that doorway.

**Spell 2:** Another way to keep evil spirits at bay is to place a black candle in the middle of a circle of salt and light the candle. It will keep the spirits away as long as it is burning.

# SPELL TO CALM A CRANKY BABY

**Items Needed**

- Candle
- Glass of water
- Lighter

To sooth and calm a crying baby, try this old Appalachian spell.

Hold a lit candle over a glass of water while concentrating on your intent (such as the baby being comfortable and calm). As you are doing this drip the melting wax into the water. Keep the glass of water containing the melted wax drippings near or under the baby's crib to keep it calm and soothed.

# TO GET RID OF A WART

**Items Needed**

- A black cat (preferably your pet) Or

- A whisker from a black cat (a found whisker)

Rub the wart with the tail of your black cat. (Please do not harm the cat). Or you can rub the whisker of a black cat on the wart. As you are rubbing the wort with the tail or whisker imagine the wart drying up and falling off. The wart is typically gone within a week.

# CHERRY TREE LOVE SPELL

**Items needed**

- Small Locke of hair
- Cherry stem on tree

**Directions**

Tie your small lock of hair around a cherry tree branch stem, as the tree blooms so will your love.

# 100TH SPELL

**What is needed:**

You

All these spells, working and conjures have one thing in common, they need you to be completed. Each one of us in the chapters before having shone you their magick, what makes them unique, now it is your turn. No one can replace what you bring to the universe, and no one should ever try. You will notice as you learn your way through this world that some spells may resonate with you and some may not, and that is you finding your way. Where you start on this journey may not be where you end up, just enjoy each step. You may also noticed that you feel drawn to add something to a spell you are drawn to, or to tweak the working to fit your needs more, if so, that is your path, this is how you learn. Never discredit your ability to achieve any of these spells in this book and more.

You are the key to all the spells.

# APPALACHIAN SUPERSTITIONS

## By Ronda Caudill

The Appalachian Mountains are steeped with superstitions brought here by our ancestors. These superstitions are still as revered as when they were when our ancestors settled these mountains. I have heard them all my life, mostly from my grandmother. I have passed them on to my children and grandchildren. I still practice the traditions to counter any bad luck such as, tossing salt over my left shoulder if spilled, crossing in front of me if a black cat crosses my path (which is several times a day since I own two black cats), and I follow all the rules of our superstitions.

### Don't Split the Pole

If you are holding hands with your significant other and come to a pole don't ever let, go of your hands. If you do this is called splitting the pole. Instead walk around the pole still holding hands. If you do split the pole, it will cause the pair to split up. However, if you do split the pole just say "bread and butter" to counter splitting the pole.

By saying "bread and butter" the couple will not split up because you cannot separate bread from the butter.

## Never Sew on Sunday

My grandmother was an exceptional seamstress and quilter. When I was a little girl, she would take old clothes that people gave her and cut them up to make clothing for myself and my sister. She would also use pieces too small for making clothing to make quilts from. She was also a very religious woman and she never sewed on Sundays. She always said that if you sew on Sunday you will have to rip out the seams after dying.

## What You Do on New Year's,
## is What You Will Do All Year

Another superstition my grandmother taught me was to be careful what you did on New Year's because that's what you would be destined to do the entire year. So, if you worked hard that day then the entire year you would be forced to work hard every day. However, if you were lazy and did absolutely nothing that day, you would accomplish nothing for the entire year. Therefore, you had to be careful and whatever you did that day must be carefully balanced.

### If You See a Cardinal, it's a Sign of Rain

My grandmother and grandfather always followed the superstitions and signs, especially when planting, tending, and harvesting the garden. They taught me that if you see a cardinal that is a sign of rain to come. So, we would prepare for rain.

### Never Enter the Garden if You Were Having Your Period

A gardening sign my family and extended family followed religiously was never letting a female in the garden if she were having her period because it would kill the plants. So, we were never allowed near the garden during that time of the month. I follow this rule religiously. I never let my daughters near the garden if they were menstruating and I never enter the garden if I am. It's better to play it safe.

### Bird Flying into a Window is a Sign of Death

If a bird flies into your window and dies (especially a black bird) this is a death omen. It is a sign that someone will soon die. My grandmother was always worried when a bird flew into the window. She swore this omen to be true from her own experiences.

### Always Come Out the Same Door You Went In

This is a superstition that I follow religiously. I never, ever go out through a door other than the one I entered. It is bad luck to go out a door from which you did not enter.

### Someone Walked Over My Grave

One eerie superstition here in the Appalachian Mountains is one of the oldest. If you get a sudden chill for no apparent reason this means someone is walking on your grave. This superstition is hard to pinpoint its origin since it is found in English, Dutch and French (among other countries) superstitions.

### If Your Ears Burn Someone is Talking About You

This Appalachian superstition is very old. The Origin is debated but most agree that it is an old Roman saying, which was originally itching or burning of the ears means someone is talking about you behind your back. Here in the Appalachian Mountains the word itching has been dropped and we say, "if your ears are burning someone is talking about you." So, beware of burning ears.

## If Your Nose Itches Company is Coming

My family has always been true believers in the superstitions that if your noses itches someone is coming to visit. This Appalachian Superstition dates back Ireland 1620.

## Knock on Wood

Knock on wood to make sure something you just talked about won't happen or to bring luck. This is a very old superstition that we here in the Appalachian Mountains believe and practice. I knock on wood a couple times a week. This superstition is common in many cultures to bring luck or ward off bad luck. Yet while the phrase "knock on wood" in Britain—has been part of the vernacular since at least the 19th century, there seems to be little agreement on its origin. One common theory is that is originated from the ancient pagan cultures such as the Celts, who believed that spirits and gods resided in trees. Knocking on tree trunks was a way to rouse the spirits and call on their protection, it was also a way of showing gratitude for a stroke of good luck. So don't forget to knock on wood.

## Sweeping Under Your Feet

If someone sweeps under your feet while you're sitting, you will never marry. This old Appalachian superstition is believed to have its origins in Africa and Voodoo brought here by the slaves. There are many other sweeping superstitions, but this is the most common one here in the Appalachian Mountains. So, keep your feet on the floor when someone is sweeping nearby.

## Covering Mirrors After a Death

Cover mirrors when a loved one dies so they won't get trapped in them. Upon the death of a loved one time literally stopped for them. A popular tradition in Victorian funeral preparations were for family members to prepare the house for death by stopping clocks and covering mirrors. Covering the mirrors was to prevent the deceased's spirit from being trapped. However, this superstition is much older than the Victorian Era; its origin lies with the Romans. Somehow this superstition and tradition found its way here to the Appalachian Mountains.

## Snapping Turtles Won't Let Go Until it Thunders

I'm not sure where this superstition came from, but it sure kept many children from playing with snapping turtles, including me. It is said that if you get bitten by a snapping turtle it won't let go until it thunders. I was told this by my grandparents, parents, and other family members.

## If You Play in Fire, You Will Wet the Bed

I heard this one all the time growing up because we were always camping, and we had a fireplace in our house that was our source of heat. So, my grandmother was constantly warning us not to play in the fire or we would wet the bed. I'm not sure where this superstition came from but many people I know were told this as children.

# APPALACHIAN SUPERSTITIONS

## By Misty

You can't say Appalachian without saying or thinking superstitions. These mountains that have been filled with immigrants from all over the world that have brought one thing with them all, their beliefs and what haunts them.

Have you ever been in one of the darkest parts of the woods, surrounded by nothing but trees, your imagination, and the stars above? This is an eerie feeling that nothing can replace, wondering if you will make it out alive in these woods that have creatures and beast you can't see during the daylight but have always been warned about. The only thing keeping you safe is the flickering embers of a fire as you all gather to hear stories of past times and what lurks in the dark. I think that some may believe this very situation is how we tell our superstitions and tales in these mountains but none I have ever handed down has been that intense or dramatic. Most of the time our superstitions and lore is ingrained in us daily, in normal everyday things we do. As you have noticed, the key to surviving these mountains is to have good luck, to not have the "devil "or haints after you and to have faith in greater things. Our superstitions are just the same with a theme of bad luck, death, and the devil. As these mountains filled with different nationalities so came different superstitions. In this melting pot, we found ways that kept us surviving in these treacherous terrains, so no one in their right mind would doubt these stories of caution handed down through our generations.

As you read, you can be the judge of whether these are worth following but my preference is with the ancestors that have survived in these hills and mountains by abiding and following them to the letter.

- A ladybug will bring you good luck.
- Watch the trees and cows for harsh weather or rain, the cows will lay down and the trees will cup their leaves up.
- You can smell rain in the air before you see it.
- A horseshoe has the open end pointed to the sky to keep the good luck in, if the two open ends are pointed down toward the ground, your luck will run out.
- Death and babies always come in threes.
- DO NOT answer your name being called, even if it is in a familiar voice, it is the devil calling you.

- NEVER whistle at night, it will call in things you don't want to be haunted by
- If you are headed out of your house and forget something and must return, it will bring you bad luck.
- Killing a writing spider will bring bad luck but if you let her stay, she will bring you good luck.
- DO NOT let a bird get your hair or you will have constant headaches.
- If you say something that you hope will happen or will not happen, knock on wood three times so you don't jinx yourself.
- DO NOT give someone something on New Years, if you do, you will be giving to them all year long.
- Beans and black-eyed peas on New Year's brings good luck.
- You exit a house the same way you came in or it is bad luck.
- If you hand someone a pocketknife, you must hand it back the same way or it is bad luck (open or closed)
- A woman on her time of the month isn't allowed in the garden, or she will kill all the crops.
- Never walk around your house with one shoe on and one shoe off, it will bring bad luck.
- If you dream of snakes, the Devil is after you.
- NEVER tell anyone your bad dream before you eat something, or it will come true.
- Plant a bush or a leafy plant near your front door to protect against haints, they have to count all the leaves before entering.
- Newspapers were placed in walls because haints must read anything before them, so it would keep them occupied instead of bothering you.
- Blue bottles or cups are put on trees or sticks to "catch" a haint, they go in and are unable to exit.
- The donkey and burro are a special animal in the mountains, it is thought to be good luck and able to ward

bad luck or evil because it was the chosen animal for Jesus and Mary.
- On Christmas Eve, 12- midnight, it is thought to be a time animals could talk and the cross on the burro's back where he carried Mary would glow.
- Burning bread would be a sign someone is coming mad.
- If a pregnant woman watches something with bad intent, something supernatural or is around something that is haunted or dark, it will mark the baby.
- Rubbing the head of a red head will bring good luck.
- Hang a mirror facing out by your front door to keep the Devil out, legend says he is so vain he will watch himself in the mirror until the sun comes up.
- Line your thresholds and windows with salt to keep out evil spirits.
- If a bird flies in your house, it is an omen of death.
- Put a penny in your shoes for good luck.
- If your nose is itching, someone is coming to visit, if your ears are burning, someone is talking about you.
- Never open an umbrella in the house or you will have bad luck.
- Smoke follows beauty.
- Fat meat will make you pretty.
- Don't let your purse touch the floor or you will lose all your money.
- NEVER point your finger at someone unless you are prepared to curse them.
- A ring around the moon means bad weather is coming or something bad.
- Wind chimes are good to keep evil spirits away.
- Never walk over a grave, it will bring bad luck and it's disrespectful.
- Idle hands are the devils' playground, so keep yourself busy.
- Copper jewelry can heal and is for good luck.

- If a black cat walks across your path, it's bad luck, unless you X it out or if you own a black cat then if one crosses your path, it is good luck.
- Brushing your hair one hundred times at night will make your hair grow and beautiful.
- You can never make anything with the first snow of the season, it would sour (such as ice cream)
- A buckeye in your pocket brings good luck.

These are some great words of wisdom to live by and I hope they bring you lots of luck and knowledge on how to outsmart the Haints and the Devil among other things

# APPALACHIAN LORE

## By Ashley

Of course, every region has many tales of things to fear or the unexplainable. Usually in my neck of the woods, it would play out like this "you know Jimmy?", "No", "Jimmy Radcliffe he was Earl's ol' boy who used to drive the school bus for your uncle", "oh yeah", "well his cousin's friend was out a-huntin' up near his house and he said he seen (insert here a wild tale you know was shine induced) and he won't go back into that holler to this day!" That my friend, is how Appalachian tall tales happen, and it occurs so naturally everyone is on the lookout and spreading mass hysteria faster than a Californian wildfire. Normally, at your local gas station it is so bad you can barely push through to buy gas and a meat stick. So, I am here to share some tales I have been pre-vied to hear from the gas station as well as my family's old farm. You will notice a trend of most Appalachian folks' stories inflict fear about the devil, demons, rabies, and mysterious predators at night. All of which are very frightening as a child going out to tend animals at night.

Some natural things we feared growing up in the mountains, that we were constantly scanning the lay of the land was for one, rabies. It was a very real fear growing up, if a wild animal wasn't acting right, it probably had rabies so you always had to be on the lookout for any small carnivore that could be scurrying about. If these randomly super speedy and abnormally strengthen animal was to catch and bite you, then you get introduced to the next level of fear…the doctor. Common city folks don't understand how this was instilled into us growing up, it was as if the sickness was scared out of us. I cannot recall how many times my family would say "if you don't start acting right or if you don't get better you're going to the doctor." By the grace of God, I was cured, and if I wasn't, I sure did act like I was in the perfect health, so I didn't get the drive to town.

Our next natural fear was snakes, and if by chance you seen one in this vast wooded area, then automatically the devil was after you and you needed to change your ways and pray. You can imagine there was a lot of praying and self-reflection time living next to the woods.

Next on the list, would be coyotes, especially at night, and if you see one in the day, then that's the double whammy, it probably had rabies. If you have a question, feel free to check a search engine of videos of rabid coyotes. We seriously took the old yeller movie to heart. It is a natural occurrence to hear a pack of them yipping and howling at night, and of course, there are stories of families of beloved animals being drug off by them.

Lastly bears, which is understandable, but the point I am laying down is the natural predators of the area we are always on our toes and watching out for the nature around us. So now I can move on to more supernatural occurrences.

A story my mom would always tell was about our lonely farm in the edge of the endless woods, late at night, we could hear a baby crying off on top of a hill behind our Johnny house. She never dared to go find the sound, but they speculated it was a bob cat or a mountain lion. Whether the sound was a phantom baby or a mountain lion, neither is a natural occurrence no one would want to come in close contact with late at night trying to make it to the bathroom. If something was unnatural we were taught to just best leave it alone and change your path. I believe to this day, this is why my mom has a weak bladder, due to all those years holding it rather than being face to face with what was making the endless screaming in the backyard. One would speculate maybe a mountain lion, but these frightening beasts were supposedly from what I was told "runned off." How exactly and why scientists were so confident how every last one was contained and moved, I cannot tell you. Yet, footage of black panthers and mountain lions will randomly surface with as much excitement as if a big foot was spotted.

    The aspects that city folks tend to not understand are how far from town you can be and how lonely you choose to be if you wanted. My farm, as I have stated, is on the edge of the woods, as in nothing behind our little plot of heaven, except for trees and mountains. At night, there are no lights behind us on this mountain. In reference, it takes a day on a four-wheeler to reach the cell phone tower on top of the mountain. No neighbors, no phone service, no roads. Of course, growing up it seemed fun to eventually wander off into the woods to explore. Random things amongst the family were markers you would seek out such as if you started early enough in the day on foot you could make it to an old abandon farmhouse deep in the woods. Again, no cars, no roadways, just randomly an outline of a small house, anyone's mind would venture to think who lived there? How did they get there? And where did they go? It's enough to keep a small child awake late at night thinking of the answers to these questions.

The incidents that followed next made a deep impression on me to never go back there again. Being that far away from home in the middle of the woods, you have to be out of there before the sun goes down or you never know what could be in there with you or how to get out. As the merry little crew made up of myself, my sister and my mom walked for hours to make it back home, keeping in mind as the evening grew, so did the light dissipate. Much like seeing sand in an hourglass or the loud ticking of a clock, yet this is a race with viability. My mom was the first to notice someone or something was following us, my sister and I were not talking much to each other, because survival of getting out kicked in. We proceeded to move faster and kept glancing back trying to get a better view of the object. The woods were eerily silent with only the sound of leaves as we stepped on them, with the occasional what sounded like wood knocking in the distances. We were only focused on quiet determination to leave whatever was following us in the woods safely behind us and to reach our farms clearing. Reassuring ourselves that it was in our minds, it was because the woods were getting darker, and it was only our imagination. Until our unwelcome trailing entity started making a new sound. That was what we deciphered as chains being dragged or moved behind us, just far enough away to get the point and enough to not be visible what was doing it. Of course, at this point we started running. The sound seemed to be keeping speed with us until finally we reached the clearing. It was the largest feeling of relief I have ever had. We finally made it home and my mom confronted my dad because he was the only person who knew we were going on our expedition. She asked him if he was trying to scare us, and he had no idea what we were talking about. To this day, we don't know for sure what it was. Over the years we speculated if it was an agitated bear that was curious and holding his ground because they are known to chatter their teeth, but the sound didn't match at all. Months later, after our encounter, a male that was hiding from the cops was discovered not far from the tree line in a tent. Although, you would think the fugitive would have laid low instead of causing alarm. None of the situations would be comforting to find out.

The thought had crossed my mind of the possibility it could have been Bigfoot. Could it have been? As humorous as it sounds, some have claimed to see the creature, on two occasions my family have seen unexplainable creatures on our country roads. Granted bears are common, but their mannerisms are different, and most country people are aware of the common bear appearance. They are at times a scary nuisance, being I have had family members who lived in a trailer that a bear broke in. Bears are fairly common, they have walked past our kitchen window, gone through our trash, and even sat on our porch nightly but the stories to follow I can assure you were not a bear.

My mother driving home witnessed a tall animal walking upright like a human with straggling body hair. She just drove home.

She didn't stop to investigate or drive back because we tend to mind our own. On another occasion, my sister and nephew saw a creature as tall as a school bus yet was pitch black and walking up right. They witnessed in pure silenced awe until they drove past and asked, "did you see that?" They turned the car around and the creature was gone. Both accounts were within five miles of each other and years apart.

Considering in each of the stories the individuals were driving, nothing can make a person feel more alone and helpless than to be traveling an old country road with no other human, nor gas station in sight. Highway and traveling tales we take seriously because it's normally a journey to get to town. A cautionary tale we constantly resist is the snow falling could hypnotize anyone driving and cause wrecks or seeing a phantom black dog means you soon will meet your doom.

My country road where my farm resides has grown over the years. At one point there were no lights and it was pitch black with only the stars or moon to light your way. As time goes on, we now have many houses that are within walking reach. So, it's not as desolate as it once was when my father was courting my ma. He would sneak to see her late at night. One faithful night my dad was walking his normal route and then after their time together he began to return down the same route to make his way back home.

When he glanced back and saw red glowing eyes following him, of course being a young teen, he was scared and began running. The red eyes which he thought maybe was the eyes of a mountain lion kept up pace and followed him all the way home. Years went by and no one confessed to it being a trick, so it remains a mystery. When he glanced back and saw red glowing eyes following him, of course being a young teen, he was scared and began running. The red eyes which he thought maybe was the eyes of a mountain lion kept up pace and followed him all the way home. Years went by and no one confessed to it being a trick, so it remains a mystery.

A plot of land on our farm was sectioned off for my great uncle, he married, had children, and started out with a trailer, then proceeded to upgrade to a house. The country dirt trail became a holler of my family members and eventually my mom and dad moved into a house beside them. One day three flaming balls of fire rolled down the dirt road, no one knew where they came from or went. Other than it was coming from my great uncle's house and then dissipate into thin air. The following years showed the odd phenomenon was foretelling because the house the flaming balls were rolling away from like tumble weeds has caught fire three times and patched up each time. It is safe to assume it will never be lived in again.

~Merry Part~
And
~Blessed Be~

# BIBLIOGRAPHY

Melungeon. (2023, March 2). In Wikipediahttps://en.wikipedia.org/wiki/Melungeon

Moonshine. (2023, April 5). In Wikipedia. https://en.wikipedia.org/wiki/Moonshine

Appalachian Music. (2023, February 21). In Wikipedia. https://en.wikipedia.org/wiki/Appalachian_music

*Appalachiosaurus*. (2023, April 14). In Wikipedia. https://en.wikipedia.org/wiki/Appalachiosaurus

Grandma Gatewood. (2023, February 14). In Wikipedia. https://en.wikipedia.org/wiki/Grandma_Gatewood

Appalachian. (2023, April 16). In Wikipedia. https://en.wikipedia.org/wiki/Appalachia

Appalachian Stereotypes. (2023, February 27). In Wikipedia. https://en.wikipedia.org/wiki/Appalachian_stereotypes

Dietrich, E. (2021, Nov 8)6 Striking Facts about the Appalachian Mountain Range.
Retrieved from https://copyfrog.medium.com/6-striking-facts-about-the-appalachian-mountain-range-aacad14978ab

Ecoclimax, (2021, May 28) The Appalachian Mountains, the Scottish Highlands and the Atlas Mounts in Africa were the same Mountain Range.
Retrieved from https://www.ecoclimax.com/2021/05/the-appalachian-mountains-scottish.html


Visit Pikeville. (2020, September 11). Hayfields and McCoy's.

Retrieved from https://visitpikeville.com/attractions/hatfield-mccoy/

Appalachian Trail Conservancy. (2010, March). Explore the A.T. Retrieved from https://appalachiantrail.org/explore/

Keppel, P. (2023). But did you know......Prohibition and Franklin County, the Moonshine Capital of the World.
Retrieved from https://blog.virginia.org/2020/05/franklin-moonshine-history/

Ward, Beth. (2017, November 21). The Long Tradition of Folk Healing Among Southern Appalachian Women
Retrieved from https://www.atlasobscura.com/articles/southern-appalachia-folk-healers-granny-women-neighbor-ladies

Engels, J. (2022, August 7). What is Bluegrass? The History and Evolution of Appalachian Music.
Retrieved from https://blueridgemountainstravelguide.com/what-is-bluegrass-the-history-evolution-of-appalachian-music/

Bonaparte, Alicia D. (2007, August). The Persecution and Prosecution of Granny Midwives in South Carolina, 1900-1940 [Doctoral Dissertation, Vanderbilt University]
Retrieved from https://core.ac.uk/download/pdf/216049364.p

# ABOUT THE AUTHORS

## ASHLEY CONNER

Ashley is born, raised, and rooted in the Appalachian Mountains, specifically the blue ridge region, along with many long lines of ancestors before her. Some family folk dabbled in wart removing, others farm and livestock remedies. Always being interested in investigating haints, hollers and folklore it became a pass time that inspired a blog radio show that Ashley co-hosted for years. That followed by traveling the United States giving magic classes, speaking on witchcraft, conducting seances and gallery readings all with the down-home Appalachian flare. Ashley has been featured in numerous media and publications, as well as wrote for a multitude of books and featured in a documentary on witchcraft called Season of The Witch. She currently resides on her little farm with her sister caring for her animals and keeping the roots of her Appalachian conjuring ways strong.

## MISTY CONNER

Misty, alongside her sister Ashley, has deep roots in the Appalachian region. Of course, they both grew up on their small farm tucked away from what they all referred to as "town" in Southwest Virginia which they still reside on. Misty is a wife and a mother that wants to pass on as much knowledge and magick as she can about where she came from before it is a forgotten history. She embraced her lineage that she knew as normal, but others knew as something special outside of these mountains. She travels the US with her Mystic of the Mountains' sisters, whether biological such as Ashley or by choice, such as Ronda, conducting seances, hosting gallery readings, lecturing, teaching classes and helping those in need. She offers the ability to use her gifts to give messages from beyond with her tarot and mediumship and preform a hands-on cleansing technique in the form of a good old mountain egg cleansing. She has been gifted with the gift of sight as it was put in the olden times and the gift to lay hands. Misty has been featured in numerous articles and publications with the current being a documentary called Season of the Witch. The documentary is for rent and purchase at fine retail outlets.

www.theconnersisters.com

# RONDA CAUDILL

Ronda L. Caudill holds a doctorate in education, is a writer, publisher, director, psychic, tasseographer, Reiki Master and owner of the haunted Nickerson Snead House in Glade Spring, VA. The Owner of Full Moon Publishing, LLC. She is part owner of Shadow Work Productions, LLC. Ronda is also a member of a paranormal group called SRS Paranormal. Ronda comes from a long line of psychically gifted women and healers whose lineage comes from Ireland and Scotland, as well as having Cherokee roots in the Appalachian Mountains (she also has an ancestor who was tried as a witch during the Salem Witch Trials). She has had paranormal experiences her entire life and began communing with the dead at age 18. Ronda has also practiced mirror scrying, table tipping, using dowsing rods, pendulums, and spirit boards for over thirty years. These are the tools that she is comfortable with being the tools used during the Victorian era, with which she has an affinity. She Travels with the Conner Sisters throughout the country conducting seances, psychic readings, witchcraft classes, etc. The magick she feels within and around her is such an integral part of her life she wants to share it with everyone. However, the most magical part of her life is her husband, children, and grandchildren.

Made in the USA
Middletown, DE
02 May 2023

29717600R00172